The great strength of this book is that it offers so much more than a primer on "membership." Really this is a book about the church in all its God-given glory and goodness and about how gracious God is in attending to our deepest desire for belonging. Jonathan Landry Cruse displays church membership as covenantally Christ-centered, pastorally beneficial, attractively necessary, spiritually nourishing, and sacrificially minded. This is the accessible guide many of us have been waiting for, and its value to the church will be immense.

—**David Gibson**, Minister, Trinity Church, Aberdeen, Scotland

In an era of frequent dechurching, we need a renewed vision for the importance and blessing of belonging to a local congregation of God's people. Thankfully, this brief book is a helpful resource —biblical, clear, and encouraging—just the kind of book I'd want to hand to a new believer or study in a new members class. With warmth and theological depth, Jonathan Landry Cruse walks us through the scriptural foundations for church membership and answers common questions we may have. I've been a church member for decades, but I was stirred by these pages to again praise God for the privilege of belonging to his body.

—**Megan Hill**, Managing Editor, The Gospel Coalition

For several decades now, this was the book that had to be written. In an age when life in the church seems optional or even implausible to increasing numbers of professing Christians, Cruse offers a warm invitation to embrace the blessings of church membership, a rich fellowship that, he rightly contends, serves to enhance our walk with God. Readers will find especially helpful his pastoral responses to common objections and misgivings.

—**John R. Muether**, Dean of Libraries and Professor of
Church History, Reformed Theological Seminary, Orlando

Jonathan Cruse has crafted simply the finest entry-level introduction to church membership. This highly accessible starter kit is biblically grounded, confessionally informed, and pastorally helpful, showing us that God instructs us to join his church, why that membership blesses us, and how we should practically live it out. I am delighted to commend this book and even more delighted to give it to people visiting my church.

—**Harrison Perkins**, Pastor, Oakland Hills Community
Church (OPC), Farmington Hills, Michigan; Author,
Reformed Covenant Theology: A Systematic Introduction

Jonathan delivers a bracing, biblical feast calling Christians back home—back to the family of faith, back to the grace of Christ, and back to the heart of God. If you're serious about getting your life on track, nurturing your faith, reversing spiritual decline, reaching out to a lost and lonely world, and securing your place in heaven, read this book. I can scarcely imagine a better resource to place in the hands of new church members.

—**Neil C. Stewart**, Senior Minister, First Presbyterian Church,
Columbia, South Carolina

CHURCH
MEMBERSHIP

BLESSINGS OF THE FAITH

A Series

Jason Helopoulos
Series Editor

Church Membership, by Jonathan Landry Cruse
Covenantal Baptism, by Jason Helopoulos
Expository Preaching, by David Strain
Persistent Prayer, by Guy M. Richard
Reformed Theology, by Jonathan Master
Reformed Worship, by Jonty Rhodes

"Jason Helopoulos has assembled a fine team
of God-centered authors who are anchored
in his Word and lovers of his church."
Sinclair B. Ferguson

CHURCH

MEMBERSHIP

JONATHAN LANDRY CRUSE

P U B L I S H I N G
P.O. BOX 817 • PHILLIPSBURG • NEW JERSEY 08865-0817

Library of Congress Cataloging-in-Publication Data

Names: Cruse, Jonathan Landry, author.
Title: Church membership / Jonathan Landry Cruse.
Description: Phillipsburg, New Jersey : P&R Publishing Company, [2024] |
  Series: Blessings of the faith | Includes bibliographical references. |
  Summary: "Reformed churches emphasize church membership. Why? Because
  membership provides all kinds of practical, spiritual blessings for our
  flourishing. This friendly overview features discussion questions and an
  extensive Q&A section"-- Provided by publisher.
Identifiers: LCCN 2023054223 | ISBN 9798887790404 (hardcover) | ISBN
  9798887790411 (epub)
Subjects: LCSH: Church membership.
Classification: LCC BV820 .C78 2024 | DDC 254/.5--dc23/eng/20240213
LC record available at https://lccn.loc.gov/2023054223

For Bob and Mary Jackson,
dear friends who bring to life the blessings of church
membership

And to him who is the head of the church
and is himself its Savior

CONTENTS

FOREWORD

It has often been said—sometimes with a sense of humor and sometimes in annoyance—that Presbyterian and Reformed churches love to do things "decently and in order." I can understand both the humor and the frustration that lie behind that sentiment. We love our plans, our minutes, our courts, and our committees. Presbyterian and Reformed folks have been known to appoint committees just to oversee other committees (reminding me of the old *Onion* headline that announced "New Starbucks Opens in Rest Room of Existing Starbucks"). We like doing things so decently that we expect our church officers to know three things: the Bible, our confessions, and a book with *Order* in its title.

But before we shake our heads in disbelief at those uber-Reformed types (physician, heal thyself!), we should recall that before "decently and in order" was a Presbyterian predilection, it was a biblical command (see 1 Cor. 14:40). Paul's injunction for the church to be marked by propriety and decorum, to be well-ordered like troops drawn up in ranks, is a fitting conclusion to a portion of Scripture that deals with confusion regarding gender, confusion at the Lord's Table, confusion about spiritual gifts, confusion in the body of Christ, and confusion in public worship. "Decently and in order" sounds pretty good compared to the mess that prevailed in Corinth.

A typical knock on Presbyterian and Reformed Christians is that though supreme in head, they are deficient in heart. We are the emotionless stoics, the changeless wonders, God's frozen chosen. But such veiled insults would not have impressed the apostle Paul, for he knew that the opposite of order in the church is not free-flowing spontaneity; it is self-exalting chaos. God never favors confusion over peace (see 1 Cor. 14:33). He never pits theology against doxology or head against heart. David Garland put it memorably: "The Spirit of ardor is also the Spirit of order."[1]

When Jason Helopoulos approached me about writing a foreword for this series, I was happy to oblige—not only because Jason is one of my best friends (and we both root for the hapless Chicago Bears) but because these careful, balanced, and well-reasoned volumes will occupy an important place on the book stalls of Presbyterian and Reformed churches. We need short, accessible books written by thoughtful, seasoned pastors for regular members on the foundational elements of church life and ministry. That's what we need, and that's what this series delivers: wise answers to many of the church's most practical and pressing questions.

This series of books on Presbyterian and Reformed theology, worship, and polity is not a multivolume exploration of 1 Corinthians 14:40, but I am glad it is unapologetically written with Paul's command in mind. The reality is that every church will worship in some way, pray in some way, be led in some way, be structured in some way, and do baptism and the Lord's Supper in some way. Every church is living out some form of theology—even if that theology is based on pragmatism instead of biblical principles. Why wouldn't we want the life we share in the church to be shaped by the best exegetical, theological, and historical reflections? Why wouldn't we want to be thoughtful instead of thoughtless? Why wouldn't we want all things in the life we live together to be done decently and in good order? That's not the Presbyterian and Reformed way. That's God's way, and Presbyterian and Reformed Christians would do well not to forget it.

Kevin DeYoung
Senior Pastor, Christ Covenant Church
Matthews, North Carolina

Introduction

BELIEVING AND BELONGING

My kids are really into puzzles right now, and I have learned that the challenge with young children and puzzles isn't so much putting them together as it is properly putting them away. We're not very good at that yet, since when we pull out a box there will inevitably be a piece missing or a piece that doesn't belong with that particular set. That's why I love putting together a brand-new one: there's no chance for missing pieces or for a rogue piece from another puzzle to have invaded. Everything has its perfect place. Every piece belongs.

What if I told you the church was God's perfect place for you in this world? Would you be surprised to learn that it's in the church where you'll find true belonging? You might protest, "Surely there are any number of places where I can find community and belonging besides the church!" I am going to push back gently and say *no*.

Okay, okay. Let me qualify a bit. Many groups, organizations, and places can offer a sense of belonging, even profound belonging. I will not argue with that. But while they can only offer a *sense* of belonging, the church offers actual belonging. This is because we were made for God. We are made in his image and made for his glory. Our purpose in this life is not attained unless we seek to live with and for him. As the ancient church father Augustine famously wrote, "Thou hast formed us for Thyself, and our hearts are restless till they find rest in thee."[1] Not only that, but we were also made for one another. Remember that in a week full of "it was good," God actually said, "It is *not* good that the man should be alone" (Gen. 2:18). We were made for God and one another—the church is where we get both.

Sometimes we look for one but not the other. We want love and friendship but on our terms, not in accordance with God's commands. Or we try to have God to ourselves, without having any sort of communal or public aspect to our faith. We weren't made for that, however. God isn't content to have us come to him as disparate individuals. He doesn't want puzzle pieces—he wants the assembled whole, the tapestry of his redemptive work around the globe and throughout the ages, to come to him and cry, "Glory!" (see Rev. 7:9–10). The church is his design for just that.

Any attempt, no matter how earnest, to find belonging contrary to God's design will leave us frustrated and ultimately empty. We have to learn the lesson that my daughter is learning: no matter which way you turn the puzzle piece, that Mickey Mouse ear does not fit with the Brachiosaurus and her family. It doesn't belong. We won't find we belong until we have found the belonging of the church. We won't fit right in this world until we are in the church.

That's a less-than-popular opinion today. In the United States, attendance at a house of worship, Christian or otherwise, has been in rapid decline, and only a small percentage of those who attend worship do so every week.[2] Over a twenty-five year period, about 40 million Americans exited the churches to which they had once belonged.[3] By and large, it would appear that formal commitment to a congregation is just something we don't care about anymore. We don't see the point.

Part of that is the emergence of a culture marked by "expressive individualism," where it is assumed that the way to find fulfillment in life is by breaking free from society's expectations (read: limitations) in favor of personal preferences. This individualism is captured by slogans like "follow your heart," "you do you," and "be true to yourself." This has created a lonely world. Shopping malls belong to a bygone era, and activities that were once sources of fellowship and community are now done in isolation. As Robert Putnam famously observed, we have begun "bowling alone."[4] The technologies that were meant to offer greater connection and community have actually become the walls we hide behind to avoid human contact.

I am saying that membership in the church is the solution to today's rampant loneliness problem, yes. But don't misunderstand me—I'm saying much more than that. The church is the answer to today's problem because it's been embedded into God's gospel answer to sin's problem from the beginning. Separation from God and one another is something that sin ushered into the world (see Gen. 3:12, 23). It is part of the curse of God. To intentionally cut ourselves off from others is a sign of ultimate folly: "Whoever isolates himself . . . breaks out against all sound judgment" (Prov. 18:1).[5] But through the work of Christ, announced in the gospel and experienced in the church, God reverses the effects of sin and brings us back to himself. We can start to live the way we were made to live: before the face of God. And we can experience our God through the community and fellowship of one another! Just as we were not *made* to be alone, we are not *saved* to be alone either! In salvation, we are not just brought to God—we are brought to his people: "Once you were not a people, but now you are God's people" (1 Peter 2:10). Believing leads to belonging.

Indeed, our faith in Christ is the foundation of our fellowship within the church. Put another way, belief is the bedrock of belonging. Incidentally, this is why doctrinal decay in churches leads to a decline in attendance and membership—after all, if we don't stand *for* anything, there is no need to stand *with* anyone. This is true in all communities, but uniquely so in the church. The bond that the church forges between her members is stronger than that offered by any other human institution or community because the shared beliefs are more significant. While fans who are cheering together for their team inside a crowded football stadium might form a visceral connection with one another, it essentially ends the moment the clock runs out and people disperse to their vehicles. In the main, when community is formed around a particular goal or interest or hobby, the bounds of that community extend no further.

The same is not true for the Christian community. The Christian community invades every aspect of our lives because what unites us—Jesus and our shared faith in him —touches upon every aspect of our lives. The church offers the most powerful kind of belonging because the belief that brings us into the church is more powerful than anything else. It's a belief about nothing less than the purpose of life. The bonds of the church, as they are anchored in God himself, provide a stability and a security that nothing else in this life can give.

I hope we are starting to see that the subject of church membership deserves more attention than we tend to give it. This is a book about finding your place in the world. This is a book about fulfilling your purpose in life, and my contention is that the church is vital to making that happen. Church membership may not be glamorous, but it's good, and it's something we desperately need.

If you are a new Christian, read this book to learn a little something of the joyful communal life you are signing up for. If you are a Christian without a church, I hope you will read this with a careful consideration of all that God has called you to when he called you to salvation, and of the blessings he offers you through membership in his bride. If you are currently a member of the church, read this book as a means of renewing your love and service for the body of Christ. If you have been hurt by the church in the past, I hope reading this book might woo you back—she is not perfect by any means, but she's the best thing on earth.

Finally, if you are not a Christian, I am glad this book found its way into your hands. And I want to thank you for reading it. Even Christians don't think about the church enough, so the fact that you have gotten this far is a real honor. Truly. But be forewarned: in the pages ahead, you will learn of the unmatched, unconditional, inexpressible love that God has reserved exclusively for the church. It's a love so amazing that you can't live without it. So you may just find yourself wanting to join a church when you're done reading!

1

THE NATURE OF CHURCH MEMBERSHIP

Recently, my wife and I were discussing our family's membership at the local YMCA. She was reminding me that we really, *really* needed to get over to the Y to put our membership on hold. Something we use every day in the dark of a Michigan winter suddenly becomes less needful when summer hits. After all, four out of five Great Lakes prefer Michigan! Here's hoping we find time to pause our membership today so that we don't keep paying for a service we're not using.[1]

When you think of church membership, perhaps you liken it to something like membership at the Y: an institution you can join or leave as you find need of its services. It's in this context that we are most accustomed to hearing the term *membership* used. But let me just put it out there right now: *church membership is not the same as membership at the YMCA.* For that matter, neither is it the same as membership at a retailer, a local book club, a museum, or a social group that serves the community, like the Lions Club or the Boy Scouts. Not even close. That's because, at bottom, membership in a Christian church is not about the relationships we forge with others or the benefits we may accrue from belonging to such a society. *Church membership is fundamentally about how we relate to God and how he relates to us.*

Another way we could say it is like this: The nature of church membership roots itself in theology, not sociology. Therefore, the blessings of belonging to the church are greater than the blessings of even the most exclusive club, because they come from God and not men. Membership at a swanky country club or the Ivy League Alumni Association says nothing about your relationship with God. Unlike these, membership in the church is of spiritual and eternal consequence. This is the nature of church membership because it is the nature of the church.

But maybe we need to remind ourselves of that. So, for starters: What is the church?

What Is the Church?

We see how important it is to belong to the church when we understand that *the church is the people of God*. There's my brief and simple definition for you. Edmund Clowney put it similarly: "The church is defined by belonging to God."[2] Though all people are God's by virtue of creation, the church is God's by virtue of salvation.

This is an extremely privileged and unique relationship —the church is God's prized treasure: "When the Most High gave to the nations their inheritance, when he divided mankind, he fixed the borders of the peoples according to the number of the sons of God. *But the LORD's portion is his people*" (Deut. 32:8–9). There's a verse to stop you in your tracks. We often think about what we get out of salvation: forgiveness, eternal life, and so on. Have you ever thought about what God "gets" out of our salvation? Deuteronomy just gave the answer: he gets the church.

And from God's perspective, that is not the raw end of the deal. He loves his church! Could God value anything more highly than that which he bought with the precious blood of his dear Son (see Acts 20:28; 1 Peter 1:18–19)? What a treasure the church is to God—and what a treasure it should be to us as well! Think of the way Peter describes it, heaping on phrase after wonderful phrase to declare that the church is "a chosen race, a royal priesthood, a holy nation, *a people for his own possession*" (1 Peter 2:9). The church is the people of God who have been called into a covenantal relationship with him (more on that in just a moment) through the gospel of Jesus Christ.

Even the meaning of the word *church* tells us something about the special status of God's people. The Greek word translated as "church" in the New Testament is *ekklesia*, meaning "assembly" or, more literally, "called-out ones." In her very name, the church is stamped as that group whom God's grace summons out of the world for special communion with him. They have been called *by* God out of the world, called *to* God in fellowship and communion, and called *for* God's glory (see also Ex. 20:2–3; Deut. 8:6–8; Eph. 1:3–6; 1 Peter 2:9–10). Therefore, to think of the church on a purely horizontal plane is to miss the point entirely. The church, in the biblical sense, could not and cannot exist without God.

To stress the point of the church's privilege, consider that the term *church* relates in a particular way to the act of worship. In corporate worship—the literal "assembly" —God's people get to do something completely foreign to the world: *meet with the living God!* Worship is where God's people really and truly fellowship with their Lord. It's a supernatural event wherein faithful worshippers "step out" of this world to experience heavenly realities (see Heb. 12:18–24). One cannot fathom a people more privileged than those who are invited to freely experience the blessing and bliss of eternity every week. The church, therefore, exists as God's prized people.

This, by the way, answers the common objection that goes something like "I'm fine with God; it's the church I have a problem with." That line is illogical to our God. Such is his love for his people, so closely has he claimed them for himself, that he takes a rejection of the church as a personal offense (see Acts 9:4).

But more needs to be said at this point regarding the nature of the church. To help us understand it better, we should consider the three primary ways the term "church" is used in the Bible. Scripture tells us that the church exists invisibly, visibly, and locally. Understanding the church from each of these "perspectives" helps us better appreciate what it means to belong to her and what a blessing it is to do so.

The Invisible Church

"Invisible church" has a sort of mysterious ring to it, wouldn't you say? That's because it is something of a mystery to us. The invisible church is the church as known only to God—it is "the Church as God sees it."[3] The Westminster Confession of Faith says that the invisible church "consists of the whole number of the elect, that have been, are, or shall be gathered into one, under Christ the Head thereof."[4] The invisible church defies the boundaries of both space and time. It is the redeemed, wherever they are and whenever they are. In other words, the invisible church is synonymous with the elect. It is made up exclusively of those people, from every time and place, who have been redeemed by Christ, regenerated by his Spirit, and restored to vital communion with him (see Eph. 1:22–23; Col. 1:18). This is "the church of God, which he obtained with his own blood" (Acts 20:28; see also Eph. 5:25).

Moreover, the invisible church is the victorious church. Members of the invisible church will someday experience the immediate presence of God, when "he will wipe away every tear from their eyes, and death shall be no more, neither shall there be mourning, nor crying, nor pain anymore, for the former things have passed away" (Rev. 21:4). They will be entirely freed from Satan, sin, and suffering.

Membership in *this* church is the most important thing in the world. That cannot be overstated. Though this little book focuses on what membership in a particular congregation is all about, those blessings all point to the joy of membership in the invisible church. And without this, nothing else matters. It does not matter if your name is on the rolls of First Presbyterian Church of Jonesburg, Missouri—what matters is if your name is on the rolls in heaven. It is "only those who are written in the Lamb's book of life" who enter glory (Rev. 21:27).

The Visible Church

The Westminster Confession of Faith helpfully defines the visible church: "The visible church, which is also catholic or universal under the gospel (not confined to one nation, as before under the law), consists of all those throughout the world that profess the true religion; and of their children."[5] We can draw out three important points from this definition: (1) the visible church is found the whole world over; (2) the visible church comprises those who profess the true faith; and (3) the visible church includes their children as well.

"Not confined to one nation." Like the invisible church, the visible church has no geographic boundaries. It is *universal*

(or "catholic," as we also confess in the Apostles' Creed). This does not mean *only* that the church of Christ is international (unlike the people of God under the old covenant). It also means, astoundingly, that by virtue of the Holy Spirit, Christians are truly united with the church the whole world over. Paul says that we are "saints together with all those who in every place call upon the name of our Lord Jesus Christ" (1 Cor. 1:2). Later, he writes that the Corinthians "are assembled in the name of the Lord Jesus and my spirit is present" (5:4). In other words, he did not feel that he needed to be in the same physical locale as the Corinthians to be, in a sense at least, gathered with them.

How amazing that Christians have real union with our brothers and sisters around the world! We should not forget them as we gather together each Lord's Day. A privilege of this global aspect of the church is that we who worship in one country can bring our brothers and sisters from elsewhere in the world before God's own throne of grace as we pray for them. The Scriptures tell us to do just that, in fact, especially for those who are persecuted. "Remember those who are in prison, as though in prison with them, and those who are mistreated, since you also are in the body" (Heb. 13:3).

"*Those [who] profess the true religion.*" If the invisible church is made up of those who *are* Christians, the visible church is made up of those who *say* they are Christian—"those throughout the world that profess the true religion." This is why many churches require what is often called a "credible profession of faith" before an individual can join them. Admittedly, just because a profession of faith *appears* genuine does not guarantee that it is. Jesus told us that "not everyone who says to me, 'Lord, Lord,' will enter the kingdom of heaven" (Matt. 7:21). We have examples of this sad reality in Scripture. Judas belonged to the twelve disciples, Ananias and Sapphira were members of the church in Jerusalem, and of the nation of Israel Paul wrote, "Not all who are descended from Israel belong to Israel" (Rom. 9:6). Not every member of the visible church is a member of the invisible one.

We should not let the reality of false professors in the midst of God's people cause us to question or doubt the viability of the church. What ultimately matters is not whether we know who are true believers but whether God does—*and he does.* "God's firm foundation stands, bearing this seal: 'The Lord knows those who are his'" (2 Tim. 2:19).

"*Their children.*" The visible church includes not only those who profess faith but also their children. That is, the church includes their children *before* the children themselves have made a credible profession. That means that membership is not only for men and women but for boys and girls too —even babies! Depending on your church background, this view may sound odd to you. How is it, you may wonder, that someone can be a member of the church before they can even be a functioning and contributing member of society?

To answer that, remember that the nature of church membership is tied to the nature of the church. The church is the people of God, and the Bible tells us that God relates to his people *by covenant*. The greatest *ekklesia* in all the Bible—that is, the most significant assembly—is when God gathered Israel before him at Mount Sinai and entered into a formal covenant with the nation (see Ex. 19–24). This national covenant was a fulfillment of the earlier promise made to Abraham, when the Lord said, "I will make of you a great nation" (Gen. 12:2). Furthermore, God told Abraham how he would bring this about, and —amazingly—it was through generational faithfulness to Abraham's lineage: "I will establish my covenant between me and you and your offspring after you throughout their generations for an everlasting covenant, to be God to you and to your offspring after you" (Gen. 17:7).

Because the promise of belonging to God was not just for Abraham but also for his children, both he and his male children received the sign and seal of the promise, namely circumcision (see Gen. 17:9–14). The sign of circumcision was the sign that someone belonged. Children belonged to the people of God. Therefore, a careful reading of the Old Testament reveals that in the community of God's people, children are not treated as second-class citizens. God gave specific instructions to ensure that they were not left in the dark concerning the significance of his covenant dealings with Israel (see Ex. 12:26–27; Deut. 6:7; Josh. 4:6–7). In the old covenant, children were treasured (see Ps. 127:3) because they were a proof of God's promise—each successive generation a sure sign that God's covenant was indeed "everlasting."

Likewise, children must be cherished in the new covenant church, and in the pages of the New Testament we see that they are! When Paul writes to churches, he anticipates that children will be present and part of the gathering (see Col. 3:20). He has no issue with calling the members of the church in Ephesus "saints" (Eph. 1:1)—and apparently no qualms about including children among those saints (see Eph. 6:1)! At the dawn of the new covenant church, Peter boldly declares, "The promise is for you and for your children and for all who are far off, everyone whom the Lord our God calls to himself" (Acts 2:39). Peter's statement seems to echo the Genesis 17:7 promise, but he also may have in mind any number of Old Testament prophecies that predicted the inclusion of children in the new covenant: Isaiah 54:13; 59:20–21; 65:23; Jeremiah 32:38–39; Joel 2:28. Remember, the church is made up of "called-out ones," and Peter is saying that the Lord often calls out not only individuals but families—entire households, which we can legitimately assume includes children (see Acts 16:15, 31–34; 18:8).[6]

Just as circumcision was once the sign of belonging to God's people, now we recognize that baptism has been given to us as "the solemn admission of the party baptized into the visible church."[7] Though the sign of the covenant has changed (see Col. 2:11–12), the nature of the covenant has not. The people whom God established by his promise of grace he still maintains and keeps by his promise of grace. The church is now "the Israel of God" (Gal. 6:16)—the undeserving recipients of his covenantal faithfulness.

So, the visible church includes both those who profess faith *and* their children, who are also called out and considered holy (see 1 Cor. 7:14). They may grow up and reject God's offer, but the offer is theirs (see Heb. 6:1–8).[8] They are members of the church until they walk away from it. Presbyterian theologian B. B. Warfield is often quoted on this score, having summarized the point well: "God established His church in the days of Abraham and put children into it. They must remain there until He puts them out. He has nowhere put them out. They are still then members of His Church."[9]

The Local Church

We have seen that the visible church is made up of those who profess faith, along with their children, anywhere in the world. The local church is the community of people who profess faith near you. It is a single expression of the visible church, whereas the visible church encompasses all local churches.

In Scripture, an instance in which "church" (*ekklesia*) stands in for the visible church would be Acts 9:31: "*The church* throughout all Judea and Galilee and Samaria had peace and was being built up. And walking in the fear of the Lord and in the comfort of the Holy Spirit, it multiplied." Here, the entire host of professing Christians is in view. Compare that with the opening of one of Paul's letters: "To *the church* of God that is in Corinth" (1 Cor. 1:2; see also 2 Cor. 1:1; 1 Thess. 1:1; 2 Thess. 1:1), or "*the church* in [Nympha's] house" (Col. 4:15), or Jesus's prophetic messages in Revelation: "To the angel of *the church* in Sardis . . ." (Rev. 3:1). In these examples, "church" means the *local* church.

Another word for the local church is *congregation*, which supposes a discernible group of people meeting in a particular place. You likely have a number of these in your town or city. Perhaps one church has a grand, historic building with a white steeple that can be spotted from anywhere in town. Maybe another meets at an empty theater that is rented out each Sunday. Maybe one worships in a renovated storefront. The local church might have a name like Christ Presbyterian Church or Converge Community Church. Some will be called "traditional," others "contemporary." Some will have plenty of programs for the community, while others might be known for their missional emphasis.

But what really defines an assembly as a local church is if it does at least these three things: it preaches the Word of God, it administers the sacraments of baptism and the Lord's Supper, and it exercises church discipline. Sixteenth-century pastor Guido de Bres wisely recognized that without these three things, you cannot have a true church. He put it like this: "The true church can be recognized if it has the following marks: the church engages in the pure preaching of the gospel; it makes use of the pure administration of the sacraments as Christ instituted them; it practices church discipline for correcting faults. In short, it governs itself according to the pure Word of God, rejecting all things contrary to it and holding Jesus Christ as the only Head. By these marks one can be assured of recognizing the true church—and no one ought to be separated from it."[10]

This effort to define a "true church" is not arrogant, or even speculative, but is necessitated by the reality of sin.[11] Just because a building has a sign that says "church" does not mean that it is a true one. "There will be false teachers among you, who will secretly bring in destructive heresies," Peter warns (2 Peter 2:1). As a result, what some call a church, Christ actually calls a "synagogue of Satan" (Rev. 2:9). Thus, these "marks" of a true church ensure that the people who gather there get the truth, the whole truth, and nothing but the truth (see 1 Tim. 3:15).

The local church is the heartbeat of the Christian's life. As Pastor De Bres says, "No one ought to be separated from it." The local church is where you invest in people and where people invest in you. The local church is God's greatest means of growing you in grace and godliness. The local church is where you go to meet with God. Because, remember, that's what church membership is all about.

Metaphors for Membership

I am convinced that an instruction manual is only as good as the diagrams it provides. That's because many of us are visual learners, especially when it comes to grasping new concepts. In his condescending kindness, God fills his Scriptures with wonderful word pictures to enhance our understanding of his truth, including what he says about the nature of the church and church membership. To help deepen our conviction that church membership is primarily theological—that is, having to do with our relationship to God before it has to do with our relationship to one another—let us consider five illustrations of the church given in the New Testament.

The Church Is a Kingdom

Christ himself connected the church with the kingdom of God in Matthew 16 when he told Peter, "On this rock I will build my church, and the gates of hell shall not prevail against it. I will give you the keys of the kingdom of heaven" (vv. 18–19). In other words, if you want to enter into God's kingdom, the gate you have to go through is the church.

The author of Hebrews echoes this line of thinking when he compares the church to the capital city of the ancient kingdom of Israel, saying that to come to the new covenant church is to "come to Mount Zion and *to the city of the living God, the heavenly Jerusalem*" (12:22). "The church is a form which the kingdom assumes," wrote famed

Princeton theologian Geerhardus Vos. "So far as extent of membership is concerned . . . it is impossible to be in the one without being in the other."[12] If the church is a kingdom, or the capital city within that kingdom, what does that make church members? Both subjects and citizens. Church members are those who are under the authority of King Jesus, who represent him in the world, and who receive the benefits of belonging to his realm.

The Church Is a Bride

The Bible also uses the metaphor of marriage to describe how the church and her members relate to Christ (see Eph. 5:25–27). The church is the bride of Christ, which means that to belong to the church is to belong to the very heart of Jesus Christ. He has given everything for you: "Husbands, love your wives, as Christ loved the church and *gave himself up for her*" (v. 25). There was no gift too great for Christ to bestow on his beloved, the church. As one theologian says, the Bible "likens the relationship of Christ and His church to that of a bridegroom and his bride. It may well be questioned whether the Word of God bestows upon the church any honor greater than that."[13] Church members who take the title of *bride* seriously will also see in it a call to persevere in fidelity to the Bridegroom. Jesus cannot be a passing fad for the sincere church member. "Forsaking all others" is the vow the Christian makes to Christ. When allured by the world and sin, when tempted to pursue comfort or conformity instead of Christ, we are called to remember our first love (see Rev. 2:4).

The Church Is a Temple

At various points, New Testament authors use old covenant temple language to describe the church. Paul says,

> You are no longer strangers and aliens, but you are fellow citizens with the saints and members of the household of God, built on the foundation of the apostles and prophets, Christ Jesus himself being the cornerstone, in whom the whole structure, being joined together, grows into a holy temple in the Lord. In him you also are being built together into a dwelling place for God by the Spirit. (Eph. 2:19–22)

Church members, when they gather together on the Lord's Day, become themselves the Lord's house (see Heb. 3:1–6; 1 Peter 2:5). By the working of the Holy Spirit, God actually dwells among his people—in a way that is even more profound and powerful than when he set aflame the temple of old (see 2 Chron. 7:1–3). What does it mean to be a church member? It means to be the dwelling place of God!

The Church Is a Body

The body is the most frequently employed metaphor for the church in the Bible (see 1 Cor. 12:12; Eph. 1:23; 3:6;

4:4; 5:23; Col 1:18; 3:15). That's why it's not uncommon to hear people speak of "serving the body" or for a church's website to have a section titled "Body Life." Although we may first think of this metaphor in terms of how the various members of the body interact and function together, when the Bible uses it, the point is principally to say something about Christ: "He is the head of the body, the church" (Col. 1:18). To be a member of a church is to acknowledge Christ as your head. This means that both the church's authority and its viability are found in him alone—he is both her leader and her life.

The Church Is a Family

Finally, the Bible describes the church as a family. Paul states this explicitly in 1 Timothy 3:15, when he says that "the church of the living God" is "the household of God" (see also Heb. 3:5–6). Implicitly, this image comes to mind anytime we encounter familial language to describe the Christian experience. This is the reason fellow Christians, and especially fellow church members, refer to one another as brothers and sisters. But this is all by virtue of how we are related to God, whose family, or "household," the church is! The blessing is profound, but it could be stated as simply as this: to have the church as your home is to have God as your Father, Christ as your Brother, and the Holy Spirit as the guarantee of your future family inheritance (see Eph. 4:6; Rom. 8:29; Eph. 1:13–14).

Conclusion

Faith in Jesus Christ changes our relationship with God. Before or apart from Christ, we are "alienated from the commonwealth of Israel and strangers to the covenants of promise, having no hope and without God in the world" (Eph. 2:12). In a word, we are not part of the people of God. "But now"—two of the greatest words in the Bible—"in Christ Jesus you who once were far off have been brought near" (v. 13). If you are a Christian, you have been brought near to God because he has made you a part of his people. He has welcomed you into the church. Membership in the church is the greatest outward expression of our privileged status as God's prized possession. It's saying something profound about the way God thinks of us, the way he views us, the way he loves us! Who wouldn't want to be a part of that?

Questions for Further Reflection

1. What do you think of when you think of the church? What are some assumptions you bring with you as you begin this book?
2. This chapter argued that the church is the people of God. What are some biblical texts that help us understand that the church is primarily about our relationship with God and not primarily about our relationship with others?

3. What is the distinction between the invisible and visible church, and why is that distinction important?

4. The Westminster Confession of Faith says that the visible church is made up of those "that profess the true religion; *and of their children.*" On what biblical basis do we claim that believers' children are members of the church?

5. Five metaphors for the church were listed in this chapter. Find two or three others in the New Testament (one scholar says there are nearly a hundred![14]). What theological significance do these other metaphors lend to our understanding of the church and church membership?

2

THE NECESSITY OF CHURCH MEMBERSHIP

I have been buying material for home projects at the same Lowe's going on seven years now. Every time at checkout, I decline the clerk's offer to join their rewards program. My reasoning is that I'm always on the last project (yeah, right). But even without the membership, I am still allowed to shop at the store. I can still receive the basic benefits of service at Lowe's without being a member. Membership may provide extra perks, but, ultimately, it has nothing to do with being able to truly participate in what is going on at the store.

Is membership in the church like that rewards club? *Must* a Christian join a church, or is it optional? That is, does a believer in Jesus Christ *have* to find a local church, submit to its leadership, and literally get his or her name recorded on the membership rolls? According to the prevailing practice of many self-identifying Christians today, the answer would appear to be no. But for nearly two thousand years, the answer that Christians gave was "Absolutely!"

Historical Precedent

A pastor named Cyprian, ministering in third-century Carthage, famously said, "You can no longer have God for your Father, if you have not the Church for your mother."[1] At the time of the Reformation, this idea was reinforced. John Calvin wrote that "there is no other way to enter into [spiritual] life unless this mother [the church] conceive us in her womb. . . . Furthermore, away from her bosom one cannot hope for any forgiveness of sins or any salvation." He goes on to say that "God's fatherly favor and the especial witness of spiritual life are limited to his flock, *so that it is always disastrous to leave the church*."[2]

The Reformed confessions codified the same conviction. The Belgic Confession (1561) states, "We believe that since this holy assembly and congregation is the gathering of those who are saved and *there is no salvation apart from it*, no one ought to withdraw from it, content to be by himself, regardless of his status or condition."[3] The beliefs of Swiss Reformed Christians were set down in the Second Helvetic Confession (1566) as follows: "We so highly esteem [the church], that we say plainly that *none can live before God which do not communicate [commune] with the true church of God*, but separate themselves from the same."[4] A final example appears in the Westminster Confession of Faith (1646): "The visible church . . . is the kingdom of the Lord Jesus Christ, the house and family of God, *out of which there is no ordinary possibility of salvation*."[5]

To be clear, these statements do not indicate that the church is the only place to *be* saved. Conversions happen anywhere and everywhere: while meeting with a friend over coffee, while attending a Billy Graham crusade, while driving alone in the car and listening to the radio, while spending the summer at a Bible camp—even while traveling on a road to Damascus. God's Spirit can find us, interrupt us, and redirect our hell-bound lifestyle at any point and at any place. God's power is not limited to the four walls of a church building, and praise him for that! But what the above statements are saying is that *once* saved, the Christian should seek to become a member of a local church. The church is the society of the saved—to act as though you do not need it is actually an indication that you may, in fact, not be saved after all.

"Unencumbered but Together"

Let's be honest: To our highly individualized, post-modern ears, suggesting that there is a correlation between church membership and salvation sounds wrong. Not only wrong, but it probably sounds arrogant and narrow-minded. We have privatized religion and morality to such an extent that even the idea of a communal obligation, or of being held to a standard that we ourselves have not set, is offensive. It flies in the face of the prevailing worldview of our time, which claims that "the ideal society is one in which people live unencumbered but together, each doing their own thing."[6]

Well, whether or not it *feels* restrictive to say that Christians must join the church is beside the point. What matters is whether it's true. If church membership has been considered necessary for the past two thousand years, we should be slow to cast it aside today. Of course, while the historical precedent of church membership is important for our consideration, we cannot build a case for it on those grounds alone. In the remainder of this chapter, I focus on what the Bible has to say about the need for church membership, since I certainly can't bind you to do something that the Bible doesn't endorse.

"Good and Necessary Consequence"

Before we dive in, let me just say that this is precisely where some people err: they claim that the Bible does not, in actuality, speak to the issue of church membership, and so it cannot be required of a believer. Although I concede that there is no chapter and verse for "Thou shalt join a local church," this does not mean the Bible is silent on the matter. The God who wrote the Bible gave us the intellect to discern its message, even when some parts of it are not spelled out as clearly as the Ten Commandments.

In the words of the Westminster Confession, "The whole counsel of God concerning all things necessary for his own glory, man's salvation, faith and life, is either expressly set down in Scripture, *or by good and necessary consequence may be deduced from Scripture.*"[7] When it comes to the topic of church membership, we are in this latter category: we are called to make "necessary" deductions about God's will for our faith and life that are drawn from the overall story of the Bible. When we approach it from this angle, we discover that there's actually quite a bit that the Bible has to say on membership in God's church and its local congregations.

A Covenantal Principle

A number of books that discuss church membership look exclusively to the New Testament for biblical support.[8] But remember, the church is the people of God, and God has had a people from the beginning of time and, therefore, throughout the whole Bible. The church is the continuation of what God began with Israel, and so looking to that covenantal nation will be instructive for us as we tackle this topic. We could start with this basic principle that is set forth in the Old Testament: *God's people are known by him, by one another, and by the world.*

The great theme of the covenant is "I will be their God, and they shall be my people" (Jer. 31:33; see also Gen. 17:7; Ex. 29:45; Zech. 8:8; Rev. 21:3). How would the people know that they belonged to God? Beginning with Abraham, God gave them a physical marker by which they would be distinguished from the rest of the world, namely circumcision. "The circumcised become members of the community with whom God has an unending relationship," says Old Testament scholar Bruce Waltke.[9] That's why Israelites referred to outsiders as the "uncircumcised" (Judg. 15:18; 1 Sam. 14:6; 2 Sam. 1:20). Without circumcision, you could not be a part of the covenant people of God. Notice how the sign of the covenant was physical and visible—it was something unmistakable to the person circumcised, and something that could be verified by others if need be (see Acts 16:3). That is all to say, in the ancient world, there was no hiding whether one belonged to God's people or not.

In today's world, it is not uncommon for people to slip into church after the announcements and slip out before the last song. People know they are there, but they don't really *know* them. The individual is able to soak in some good music, hear some profitable teaching, and get a spiritual tune-up—but not to commit in any formal way to the people who are gathered there. Nothing like that was possible in the old covenant: "If a stranger . . . would keep the Passover to the Lord, let all his males be circumcised. Then he may come near and keep it; he shall be as a native of the land" (Ex. 12:48). Formal membership *into* the nation was a prerequisite for full worship *with* the nation.

Belonging matters. This principle plays out in sections we often skip over when reading our Bibles: the long lists of really hard-to-pronounce names. For example, Numbers 1 and 2 are largely taken up with a census that records the size of each tribe of Israel, followed by a schematic for where they should be positioned in the camp as the nation backpacked its way to the promised land. From the Israelites' perspective, the census was an important opportunity to commit themselves to the Lord and to their fellow Israelites (particularly because it helped them prepare for eventual war!). It was a way of signing up, or being all in.

The first several chapters of Chronicles include a list of literally hundreds of names in a record of Israel's genealogies. For a history book written during the time of exile, it was important to make the people know that God had not forgotten them. In fact, their names were written in his book! Likewise, the names of those who returned to the land from exile are listed in Ezra 2 and Nehemiah 7. Passages like these that initially read as dry as dirt suddenly come to life when you realize what God is communicating to his people by recording their names. He is speaking to each and every individual of the nation and saying, "I know you, and I have a place for you." In the Bible, therefore, it is clear that true faith is never private. God's dealings with his covenant people proved that they were known by him, by one another, and by the world.

New Testament Presuppositions

This principle, which undergirded the old covenant people of God, continues in the church. The New Testament writers never come out and say that church membership is necessary. Rather, they assume that church membership is necessary, because formal membership in the covenant people of God has *always* been necessary. Since nothing had changed, nothing needed to be explicitly stated. So what we find in the New Testament instead are little snapshots, or evidences, that prove church membership was both presupposed and practiced.

Consider how Acts often describes the growth of the church. It comes not only with the preaching of the gospel and conversion (which would add an individual to the *invisible* church) but also with the initiatory rite of baptism (a public activity that would add an individual to the *visible* church). "So those who received his word were baptized, and there were added that day about three thousand souls" (Acts 2:41; see also 8:12; 10:44–48; 18:8). In the same way that circumcision was required to enter the official people of God, baptism is now required.

Here's an interesting question to consider: How did the church know that those who were added to their number were "about three thousand"? Did they make the new converts fill out an entrance form before joining the church? Did they have someone taking attendance? We are not told the logistical details, but we can gather that entrance into the church was both public enough and organized enough that even some statistics could be gathered (see also Acts 4:4)! The New Testament knows nothing of a privatized Christianity—rather, it presupposes a public faith involving formal membership into the people of God through baptism.

Furthermore, as we considered briefly at the close of the last chapter, the various metaphors that the Spirit-inspired writers of the New Testament use to describe the church presuppose membership. A kingdom is made up of subjects, and a city consists of citizens. The nature of these civic societies requires formal declarations of belonging that determine a whole host of things, like who pays taxes, or who is eligible to receive access to governmental programs —and the New Testament says that the church is like *that*. Likewise, the church is described as a family, and families are discernible and definite units of people, known even to outsiders by things like their appearance, their name, and their place of residence. The church is also likened to a body comprising various body parts. One of the first things our children learn are the parts of their body. If my two-year-old knows her head, shoulders, knees, and toes, the church should be able to name the various members that make up its body too.

Ecclesiastical Practice

Another thing becomes evident when we consider passages in Scripture that pertain to the church: her *practice* demands formal church membership. In other words, if we take seriously what the New Testament says, a healthy, properly functioning church cannot be conceived apart from membership.

Peter's exhortation to elders to "shepherd the flock of God *that is among you*" (1 Peter 5:2) assumes that congregations had clear-cut boundaries. Elders knew those who belonged to them and over whom they must exercise oversight. Likewise, Hebrews instructs believers to "obey *your* leaders and submit to *them*" (Heb. 13:17). They are not to obey *any* leaders but rather to obey *their* specific leaders. Paul says something similar: "We ask you, brothers and sisters, to respect those who labor *among you and are over you* in the Lord and admonish you" (1 Thess. 5:12). How did they know which leaders those were? How did they know to whom they had this obligation? The language employed in the Scriptures regarding how the laity and the leadership are to interact requires commitment and a formal relationship, both of which we find in church membership.

When Paul writes to a church, he often addresses particular issues that are going on among the members of that church. Take Philippians 4:2 as just one example: "I entreat Euodia and I entreat Syntyche to agree in the Lord." While we can extrapolate a generic principle here—that Christians should be at peace with one another—it's in the context of the local church where the rubber meets the road, so to speak, and where our principles are put into practice. It's not enough for Euodia or Syntyche to assent that being at peace is a good thing. They actually had to make peace *with each other*. A biblical church is not filled with people who simply assent to lofty principles of do-goodery; it's made up of people who commit themselves to *doing good to one another* (see Heb. 10:24). Regarding the many "one another" commands in Scripture, Wayne Mack writes that "a Christian who is not committed to a local church and rarely meets with the same group of believers cannot fulfill these commands. Not only that, but our contact with other people must be so regular that we're able to know their needs, their struggles, their joys, and their burdens. These 'one another commands' require intimate, rather than casual, interpersonal relationships."[10]

Consider also that the final step in church discipline, as prescribed by Jesus himself, is excommunication (see Matt. 18:17). Paul provides some more detail in 1 Corinthians 5, but the essence of excommunication is in the name: it means to be out ("ex") of fellowship ("communion"). For someone to be *out* implies that they were once *in*. In *what*, exactly? An amorphous, anonymous group of people? Clearly not. The church is not like after-school pickup basketball, where whoever happens to show up that day is "in." Excommunication teaches us that the church is a clearly defined group of people governed by God's Word and that there are consequences when that Word is not heeded.

Conclusion

When taken all together—the covenantal principle, New Testament presuppositions, and ecclesiastical practice —the historical precedent is well-founded: "there is no ordinary possibility of salvation" outside the local church. Note that the Westminster Confession includes the word *ordinary*, which suggests that there may be times in God's providence when people are hindered from joining a church (for example, the thief on the cross). But that is the exception, not the norm. Since the biblical evidence is so compelling, we should make not only church attendance but also church membership a priority in our lives.

Let me be clear: the goal is not simply to get your name on the rolls of a congregation. I am after not mere membership but meaningful membership. We will unpack what that looks like in the remainder of the book. But before we can make our membership meaningful, we need to see that it matters. The Bible shows that it matters to God—does it matter to you? If you are a Christian, it really must. Your relationship to the church is a barometer for your spiritual condition. After all, a Christian is one who claims to love Christ—but how can we say we really love Christ if we don't love what he loves? If we love someone, we love what they love. If we love Jesus, we will love his church (see John 13:35). Have you considered that there is nothing in this *entire* world that Jesus loves more than the church? Literally nothing. And in the next world, Christ's love for the church will be second only to his love for the Father and the Spirit. That's why the hymn lyric is so profound as it describes the depths of Christ's love:

> From heav'n he came and sought her
> To be his holy bride;
> With his own blood he bought her,
> And for her life he died.[11]

Christ showed his love for us by dying for the church. Now he calls us to show our love for him by joining her. Is that too much to ask? Not at all. In fact, it would be a great privilege to do so for such a great Savior. As a fellow pastor once said, "If you want to know what someone thinks of Christ, ask them what they think of the church."[12] The church is the manifestation of Christ on earth (see Eph. 1:22–23), and it's the way we experience him until we are in heaven face-to-face with him. How can I claim to love Christ if I'm not willing to commit myself to his body, the church?

If someone were to ask you why you joined a local church (assuming you have), this would be a great answer: "I joined the church because the Bible tells me to join the church." That's what we have considered together in this chapter. But here's an even better answer: "I joined the church because I love Jesus."

Questions for Further Reflection

1. How do you react to the idea that church membership is necessary, before and after reading this chapter?
2. Discuss the historical teaching we saw in this chapter that one could not claim to be a Christian or have hope for salvation if one did not belong to a local church.

3. What was the covenantal principle set forth in this chapter? How does that relate to your understanding of the church today?

4. How do the various "one another" commands assume a system of formal membership within the church? What does this have to do with Philippians 4:2? Search the New Testament epistles for some of the "one another" commands. How can you put them into practice this week?

5. How does church membership express our love for Jesus?

3

THE BENEFITS OF CHURCH MEMBERSHIP

We saw in the previous chapter that church membership is a biblical necessity. Remember that whatever God requires of us is always for our good, a truth that includes our membership in a local church. Church membership brings with it serious responsibilities: demands on our time, expectations of our talents, restrictions on our conduct, and more. But it also brings immense blessings —perks better than rewards points, discounted rates, or any other incentive offered by a human institution.

What are these blessings? Three stand out as the most important. Church membership

- protects its own from the threats of sin and Satan,
- silences doubts and instills confidence in the hearts of its members, and
- fosters a lasting, soul-satisfying community that can be found nowhere else on earth.

Or, put another way, membership in God's church provides security, assurance, and companionship—all of which we humans desperately need. Remove any of these, and life quickly becomes a miserable chore. We are weak, doubting, and lonely creatures, and thus church membership answers our frailty with blessings tailor-made by our loving heavenly Father, who "knows our frame" (Ps. 103:14).

Security through Spiritual Oversight

Church members are blessed by the spiritual oversight that they receive from leaders within the church, who are normally called "elders."[1] Now, this first blessing might sound more like a burden. I get it. It's hard to get any twenty-first-century Westerner behind the idea that submission to authority is inherently good. How can I possibly be "the master of my fate" or "the captain of my soul" if I belong to a church?[2] Well, I can't—and that's a good thing! Why? Why is church authority a blessing?

Here's the simple truth: left to ourselves, we would quickly make a spiritual wreck of our lives. God, knowing this, not only graciously brings us into a supportive community but also gives us leaders within that community who have a vested interest in our spiritual welfare. As the apostle Paul tells us, to ensure that the church is sound in doctrine, pure in conduct, and unified in purpose, Christ himself gave her leaders (see Eph. 4:1–16). The nineteenth-century Scottish ruling elder David Dickson writes, without exaggeration, that "the eldership, under some form or other, is absolutely necessary for a healthy and useful Church."[3] Let's consider the twofold blessing that church leadership provides for those under their care.

Protection

Think first of the blessing of protection that comes from having spiritual oversight. If you are a member of a local church, what does it mean for you specifically? It means that Christ has appointed men with a mission to protect you from Satan and his attacks.[4] Consider the way one New Testament author describes the ministry of elders in the church: "Obey your leaders and submit to them, *for they are keeping watch over your souls, as those who will have to give an account.* Let them do this with joy and not with groaning, for that would be of no advantage to you" (Heb. 13:17).

The work of an elder is *difficult*. They are "keeping watch" over the souls in their care, the verb there literally meaning "to lose sleep." The sentry gives up sleep in order to protect the city, so that the citizens can slumber softly and soundly in the comfort of their beds. The work of pastors and elders does not remove the important responsibility of our own personal watchfulness (see Matt. 26:41), but the prayers, exhortations, and encouragement of church leaders is like air support that comes in from above to bolster the infantry.

Another way elders protect the people is actually by protecting the pastor. They have a charge to guard the conduct and ministry of the pastors and preachers within a local congregation. By doing so, they ensure that the sheep are being faithfully shepherded through both the public (preaching) and private (counseling and discipling) ministries of the pastor. Thus, elders should be the ones listening most intently to every sermon and watching most carefully how a pastor interacts with his congregants.

The work of an elder is also *dangerous*. To stand up as a leader in the church puts a target on one's back for the devil. The Puritan pastor Richard Baxter warned would-be elders, "Take heed to yourselves, because the tempter will more ply you with his temptations than other men. . . . He beareth the greatest malice to those that are engaged to do him the greatest mischief."[5] Beyond the attacks of the Evil One is the coming judgment of the Holy One: "Not many of you should become teachers, my brothers, for you know that we who teach will be judged with greater strictness" (James 3:1). Leaders in the church volunteer to face a stricter judgment on the last day—such is their care and concern for the church.

Indeed, the elder *willingly* enters all these difficulties and dangers; Peter speaks of under-shepherds as those who do their work "not under compulsion" (1 Peter 5:2). When you become a member of a church, you receive the care of men who are willing to do spiritual battle on your behalf. Men who expose themselves to dangers and difficulties in order to protect you and promote your peace, welfare, and security. What is that if not a blessing?

Now, will church leaders execute their calling perfectly? No. They will miss things, misjudge situations, and offer imperfect counsel. More tragically, the Bible warns us that some church leaders will intentionally abuse their authority to harm those under their care (see Matt. 7:15). In this way, God's intended blessing can be morphed into something closer to a curse. But the reality of imperfect leaders is not a valid reason for shirking submission to church authority altogether. God knows better than anyone how sinners can twist good things (like leadership) into bad things, and, knowing this, he still has given us leaders and has called us to submit to them. We do this with the faith that our ultimate soul-care is in the hands of the Good Shepherd, Jesus Christ, and that he *does* overrule the sin of his under-shepherds, so that they are still instruments of his protection and provision.

Correction

While elders are to labor as best they can to prevent their flock from falling prey to the wiles of Satan, such is the pull and power of sin that this protection is not always enough. At times, correction is required instead. This is what we would call *church discipline*. We tend to think of discipline in purely negative terms, and hearing the word conjures up thoughts of shunning and shaming. But the church has historically had a very positive view of discipline, affirming that it exists to restore people from sin, preserve the true doctrine of the church, and keep God's people pure in the eyes of the world.[6] In other words, it is *only* a good thing! Let's keep things straight: it is *sin* that makes us miserable, not church discipline. Things that draw us away from sin exist to restore joy in our lives.

And yet it's a privilege reserved for members of a local church. This is not to suggest that every church member, when they fall into sin, heeds the admonition of their elders and fully repents. But it is to say that when someone has not joined a church and made a formal declaration of submission to the elders, they are far less likely to feel an obligation to listen to an elder's warnings.

I have seen this play out during my time as a pastor. Once, a dating couple was visiting my church for several months, and, as they were very excited about the preaching and the fellowship, they wanted to meet with me to talk about getting more involved. At that meeting, I discovered that the woman was in the process of divorcing her husband and that this couple was living together. I explained that this was contrary to biblical instruction and that, before we talked about their further involvement with our church, they would need to stop living in sin. The man rebuffed me with a line akin to "I'm a grown man. I don't need the church acting like my mom and telling me how to live my life." They never returned to the church. About two years later, I bumped into the man in town. He had a baby girl with him—the couple had gotten pregnant, and the mother abandoned the baby and the father, leaving them for another man. It was a sad encounter and a powerful picture of the dangers that can come when we do not submit ourselves to the oversight that God provides through his church.

Contrast that with the individuals who are bound to the church in formal membership. Sometimes they also will run at the first sign of discipline, true enough. But I have witnessed the blessed inverse as well: members who seek the elders out and say, "I have messed up. I have sinned greatly. And I need your help." They understand that, although it's unpleasant, the correction of the church is something they desperately need—and they are ultimately grateful for it. In my experience, it is the members who believe that the church leaders are *for* them who are most ready to submit to the process of discipline.

A pastor friend of mine shared with me a moving story that well illustrates the point. A young man had been addicted to pornography for years. He knew the habit was incompatible with his Christian faith, but nothing he did seemed to work. His pastor suggested that he confess his sin formally to the elders and submit to the consequences that might result from such a confession. He did so, and he was initially shocked at the elders' decision that he be barred for a time from partaking of the Lord's Supper. After all, he came for their help, and they were punishing him instead! But his pastor wisely explained that discipline is a means of *grace*. If he wanted help, this was one of the ways to get it. Six months later, he came back to the elders in tears, thanking them for the love they showed him by placing him under discipline. He hadn't looked at pornography in months. They asked him how the discipline had changed his perspective, and he said, "Every week as the bread and wine came by and I wasn't permitted to partake, I got the most powerful wake-up call. I realized this could be my future: not being able to have Jesus. I knew then that nothing was worth keeping me from him any longer." This young man learned the grace of God's discipline.

Similarly, as you try to frame church discipline as a blessing, remember that the least pleasant aspects of discipline are often borne by the elders and not by the erring church members. Elders are called to sacrificial, arduous labor on behalf of the sheep. They cannot ignore sin in their members' lives. Far from it—they have a God-given responsibility to go reclaim those members from sin. Reformer Martin Bucer, in his book *Concerning the True Care of Souls*, writes, "Faithful ministers of Christ are not to give up lightly on anyone, as long as people are still people. . . . [Christ] desires that they should be sought where they are scattered, and sought with such seriousness and diligence that one should be ready to be all things to all men, as dear Paul was, and even to hazard one's own life, as the Lord himself did, so that the lost lambs might be found and won."[7] Shepherding the sheep is no easy task, but elders are called to "suffer everything from them and for their sakes, until we have placed them back again in the true and complete communion of the church."[8] What a kindness from the Lord to place such shepherds over members of the church, since we, like sheep, will go astray.

Assurance through the Sacraments

Another significant blessing of church membership is access to the sacraments of baptism and the Lord's Supper. The Belgic Confession summarizes well the benefit that the sacraments are to God's people: "We believe that our good God, mindful of our crudeness and weakness, has ordained sacraments for us to seal his promises in us, to pledge his good will and grace toward us, and also to nourish and sustain our faith."[9] Jason Helopoulos is absolutely right to conclude that "God's kindness radiates through this gift of the sacraments."[10] In these two simple acts, God has given the church impressive weapons with which to fend off the great enemies called spiritual doubt and anxiety.

Sadly, in recent years the sacraments have been increasingly unhitched from the local church, and so the idea that they should be reserved for members is bizarre to many. Maybe you have heard of people being baptized at the lake during summer camp (or even in their hot tub on the back deck!)[11] or of individuals celebrating the Lord's Supper alone in their homes with whatever elements they might have on hand—even cookies and soda instead of bread and wine! But the sacraments were never meant to be severed from the local church, in either their meaning or their administration.

Baptism

In the Reformed and Presbyterian (and, I would argue, biblical) conception, it's impossible to have church membership apart from baptism. It belongs solely to the those who have joined the church. In the words of the Westminster Larger Catechism, "The parties baptized are *solemnly admitted into the visible church*, and enter into an open and professed engagement to be wholly and only the Lord's."[12] This makes good sense. Baptism replaced the old covenant sign of circumcision, and there was no way for someone to become a part of the nation of Israel without receiving that sign (or, for a woman, without being related to someone who received the sign). No one could participate in the privileges of the old covenant apart from circumcision (see Gen. 17:10; Ex. 12:48). Likewise, in the New Testament, entrance into the church is tied to baptism (see Matt. 28:19; Acts 2:41).

It is a distinct privilege of church membership to know the sweet assurances that come with baptism. In the words of the Heidelberg Catechism, God "assure[s] us by this divine pledge and sign that we are spiritually cleansed from our sins as really as we are externally washed with water."[13] Baptism identifies us with Christ in our death to sin and our resurrection to newness of life (see Rom. 6:3–4); it pictures the wrath of God passing over us (see 1 Peter 3:20–21); it promises the cleansing power of the Holy Spirit (see Acts 22:16; Titus 3:5); and it is a symbol of our communion with the other members of the church (see 1 Cor. 12:12–13). Put another way, baptism is a sign and seal of the *covenant promises* of God, and those promises are reserved for the *covenant people* of God. Members of the local church have a sweet confirmation in the sacrament that the promises are theirs. Christians who refuse such membership, or who abuse the sacrament by privatizing it, lack that assurance.

The Lord's Supper

The meaning of the Lord's Supper is also deeply connected with the church community, not only in its proper administration but in its theological significance. It is not merely a meal we partake of to remember the death of Christ for our sins, but it is a spiritual means of tightening the bond Christians have with one another. In other words, to try to have the Lord's Supper as part of your private devotions at home is to miss the point altogether.[14] It's in the name, after all: *Communion*. The communion that we experience in the Lord's Supper is not only with Christ but also with his church. Paul writes, "Because there is one bread, we who are many are one body, for we all partake of the one bread" (1 Cor. 10:17).

Reformer John Calvin wrote very passionately about this horizontal nature of the Supper, and he is worth quoting at length:

Now, since [Christ] has only one body, of which he makes us all partakers, it is necessary that all of us also be made one body by such participation. The bread shown in the Sacrament represents this unity. As it is made of many grains so mixed together that one cannot be distinguished from another, so it is fitting that in the same way we should be joined and bound together by such great agreement of minds that no sort of disagreement or division may intrude. . . . What sharper goad could there be to arouse mutual love among us than when Christ, giving himself to us, not only invites us by his own example to pledge and give ourselves to one another, but inasmuch as he makes himself common to all, also makes all of us one in himself.[15]

What does this mean for the church member? Just as baptism is the means of our solemn admission into the visible church, the Lord's Supper is the continual confirmation that we *belong* to the church—it tells us we are in the right place! Our sin tells us otherwise. Sin casts doubt on our standing before God, trying to squelch our enjoyment of belonging to God's covenant community, whereas the Supper exists, in part, to enhance our delight of belonging to God and his people. I was once counseling a young man who was hesitant to make a profession of faith because he struggled with assurance of salvation. He reasoned that he shouldn't join the church until he no longer had doubts about the state of his soul. He was surprised to hear me tell him that this is precisely *why* he should make profession and start coming to the Lord's Supper: it reminds us that we do indeed belong to the church, and in belonging to the church we belong to Christ himself! Would you want to go through your Christian life without that frequent confirmation and assurance? Of course not, which is why church membership is so crucial.

Companionship through the Communion of Saints

As private and introverted as we often are, we were made to belong to a community, and perhaps we need that reminder today more than ever before. In May 2023, the Surgeon General of the United States, Vivek Murthy, issued a warning to the American public and a call to action to fight what he named an "epidemic of loneliness and isolation." He argued that "in recent years, about one-in-two adults in America reported experiencing loneliness. And that was before the COVID-19 pandemic cut off so many of us from friends, loved ones, and support systems, exacerbating loneliness and isolation. Loneliness is far more than just a bad feeling—it harms both individual and societal health."[16] People are also realizing this in light of the rise of the so-called religious "nones"—those with no religious affiliation. In a tragic opinion piece for the *Washington Post*, columnist Perry Bacon Jr. admitted, "I'm currently a 'none' or, more precisely, a 'nothing in particular.' But I want to be a something."[17] We need God, *and* we need one another—the church is where we get both.

Even more to the point, we could say that in the church we get God *through* others. God mediates his presence to us through the presence, words, and actions of our fellow church members. The German Lutheran minister and martyr Dietrich Bonhoeffer knew this reality better than most. Writing about his time as a professor of an underground seminary in Hitler's Germany, he said, "The physical presence of other Christians is a source of incomparable joy and strength to the believer."[18] Have you experienced this? In a variety of contexts—crying on the floor with a dad who just lost a child, sitting next to a wife in court as her husband gets arraigned, facilitating the confession of adultery from one spouse to the other—the response I've received has been a simple and heartfelt "Thank you for *being there.*" Bonhoeffer goes on to explain why Christian companionship is so critical: "The prisoner, the sick person, the Christian in exile sees in the companionship of a fellow Christian a physical sign of the gracious presence of the triune God. . . . Christianity means community through Jesus Christ and in Jesus Christ."[19]

This means that the Christian called into a covenant community has a responsibility to reflect and represent Christ to their fellow brother or sister. Thus, Christian companionship is never a means unto itself. Rather, it is "a mechanism for Christian growth, a spiritual radar (with mutual alarms to sin), and a means to stir us up to love and good works."[20] In other words, the church is not a place where Christians happen to be together—it's a place where we are called *to be Christians* to and for one another. Man's purpose is to glorify and enjoy God, and within the church, fellow members help one another attain that end. We are to "exhort one another every day, as long as it is called 'today,' that none of you may be hardened by the deceitfulness of sin. For we have come to share in Christ, if indeed we hold our original confidence firm to the end" (Heb. 3:13–14). Just as Adam needed Eve not only for friendship but also for the fulfillment of his God-ordained calling, Christians need the church to attain the purpose for which they were made. It's therefore no wonder why James Bannerman, a nineteenth-century Scottish preacher, once wrote, "According to the arrangement of God, the Christian is more of a Christian in society than alone, and more in the enjoyment of privileges of a spiritual kind when he shares them with others, than when he possesses them apart. . . . In the fellowship of the Church . . . the believer is in a more eminent sense a believer, than apart from them."[21]

Now, someone might protest, is formal membership actually necessary to receive these benefits of Christian communion? I would argue yes, just as I would argue there are benefits to marriage that aren't guaranteed in cohabitation. The legal and public nature of marriage calls couples to a higher degree of fidelity and likewise offers more stability and security within the relationship. This does not suggest that cohabitating couples do not love each other, but it is to say that there is less binding them to that love than a married couple who has made vows.

Similarly, Christians are called to love all, but that love is demanded and fortified in a greater way within the context of membership in a local church.

For example, at my church I exhort the entire congregation to make this promise when a new member joins: "As [name] is received into full communion in the church, the whole congregation is obligated to receive [him/her], for in Christ we are members of one another. Christ claims this [brother/sister] as his own and calls you to serve [him/her] in love. Therefore, you ought to commit yourself before God to assist [name] in [his/her] Christian nurture by godly example, prayer, and encouragement in our most precious faith and in the fellowship of believers."[22] The congregation then raises their right hands and, when asked if they will make this promise, gives a thunderous "We do!" It's a powerful moment, and my hope is that each member of the church remembers it when they are struggling in their Christian walk. They do not walk alone. A church member never does. When you are in the throes of suffering or sorrow, it's hard to overestimate the help of having an entire congregation of God's people praying for you.

Joining a church utterly transforms our station in life. The church expresses the truth of Psalm 68: "Father of the fatherless and protector of widows is God in his holy habitation. God settles the solitary in a home" (vv. 5–6). Those who have experienced abusive families now find one marked by God's love. Those who have struggled long with loneliness enjoy lasting fellowship. The barren are made spiritual parents to a whole host of children. Widows find the compassion and provision of an entire community. This is all through the powerful unifying work of the Holy Spirit. Richard Baxter once described the blessings of the church like this: "When I am poor in my own body, I am rich in millions of others, and therefore rich in mind: When I am sick and pained in this narrow piece of flesh, I am well in millions whose health is mine: and therefore I am well in mind: when I am neglected, abused, slandered, persecuted in this vile and perishing body, I am honoured in the honour of all my brethren, and I prosper in their prosperity, I abound in their plenty, I am delivered in their deliverances; I possess the comfort of all the good which they possess."[23]

Undoubtedly, Baxter is speaking of a mystical reality, something that is true of those who belong to the invisible (or universal) church. But it is through the Christian community of the local church that those spiritual realities come home to us in flesh-and-blood ways. Would Christians today continually absent themselves from worship or isolate themselves from the church if they realized that these sorts of blessings could be known and felt within the community of God's people?

Conclusion

Even if we were to explore the many other blessings of belonging to the church through formal membership, do we need to say more to prove its goodness? Church membership affords unmatched, unparalleled, and unrivaled benefits. The church member has personal spiritual security guards in the elders; spiritual nourishment in the sacraments; and spiritual companionship, camaraderie, and encouragement in the family of faith. These are truly *blessings* —undeserved gifts from God that he has given in love to those who join themselves to his church. Are they yours?

After this survey of blessings, a question comes to my mind that was initially asked by the psalmist: "What shall I render to the LORD for all his benefits to me?" (Ps. 116:12). I imagine we will spend all eternity learning and living out the answer to this question. But as for how we should respond to God for the benefits of church membership, we don't need to wait until then. We can start right now, and chapter 4 will show us how.

Questions for Further Reflection

1. Beyond those listed in this chapter, what other blessings of church membership can you think of?
2. What kind of spiritual oversight does a healthy church provide? Why is this so important for us?
3. What is the point of the sacraments? Have you ever experienced how baptism or the Lord's Supper can encourage and strengthen a believer?
4. What does it mean that Christian companionship is not a means unto itself? What is the greater purpose of the Christian community?

5. In what ways does church membership allow us to share in the joys and sufferings of others? Why is that so important?

4

THE RESPONSIBILITIES OF
CHURCH MEMBERSHIP

If church membership is fundamentally a blessing from God, why are so many skeptical, opposed, or noncommittal? A 2023 article for the *Atlantic* suggests one possible reason for the rapid decline of church membership and attendance over the last twenty-five years: "A vibrant, life-giving church requires more, not less, time and energy from its members. It asks people to prioritize one another over our career, to prioritize prayer and time reading Scripture over accomplishment. This may seem like a tough sell in an era of dechurching. If people are already leaving—especially if they are leaving because they feel too busy and burned out to attend church regularly—why would they want to be part of a church that asks so much of them?"[1] It's true. The church asks a lot of her members. We are busy people, with a lot of commitments and far less time—can we afford to serve in the way the church expects of her members? Are we willing to reprioritize our schedules to make it happen?

That's a big ask. I get it. But before we could ever appropriately respond to the demands God has of us, we need to meaningfully reflect on all that he has done for us first. This is apostolic logic: the New Testament epistles first tell us what God has done (the indicatives of the gospel) before they command what we must do (the imperatives of the gospel). I've tried to lay out the indicatives in the previous chapters of this book. So, let's briefly review what we've considered about the church thus far.

The church is the people—indeed, the *special* people —of God, who belong to him by virtue of the crucifixion and death of his dear Son (see Acts 20:28). Those who know salvation through Christ are called to experience that salvation through the privilege of belonging to a local church. That comes with immense blessings, like pastors and elders who shepherd us away from spiritual danger, sacraments that confirm God's promises to us, and fellow believers who encourage us in our faith. God's love in giving us the church should be met with our love in serving that church. Once the gospel clicks, service in the church goes from a chore to a delight. John Newton wrote a hymn that captures this pattern:

> Our pleasure and our duty,
> Though opposite before;
> Since we have seen his beauty,
> Are joined to part no more:

It is our highest pleasure,
No less than duty's call;
To love him beyond measure,
And serve him with our all.[2]

Chapter 3 considered the benefits of church membership, and now we turn to its responsibilities. But don't make too strong a distinction here—even these responsibilities are turned into blessings for us as we engage in them with hearts of faith, hope, and love. Funny how it works with God: even those things that are our duty become our delight.

So, how might we serve God with our all in the local church? What are the responsibilities and expectations that are placed upon those who join the church through membership? Let's consider them under four general headings.

Showing Up

The very first responsibility is the most fundamental, and it's something so obvious that it's almost embarrassing to say: we must *show up*. Joining a church means you are committing to participate in the various ministries of that church, the most important of which is actually going to church on Sunday! The Bible makes this clear:

> And let us consider how to stir up one another to love and good works, *not neglecting to meet together*, as is the

habit of some, but encouraging one another, and all the more as you see the Day drawing near. (Heb. 10:24–25)

When we choose not to gather with God's people for worship, it is never a decision we can make apart from our relationship with and responsibility to God. We forget that, though. Consider when you decide to stay home from church one day because you just don't feel like going. Maybe you've had a busy weekend. Maybe there's an opportunity to travel with friends, or maybe there's a sporting event for the kids. Whatever your reason, realize that it is none other than God who has arranged through the elders of your local church to call you to worship—and you have rejected *his* call. To say that our fundamental responsibility is to show up isn't to set the bar low regarding our part in corporate worship. Far from it—it's setting the bar high, for it sets it at obedience to almighty God.

Enter His Courts!

In a day of livestreaming, it's also important to underscore that the showing up we're talking about here is the in-person kind, not the virtual-viewer kind. Virtual church is not church. Livestreamed worship is no substitute for the real thing—"corporate" worship comes from the Latin for "body" (*corpus*), after all.[3] Virtual church prevents you from participating in the elements of worship and from blessing your brothers and sisters in the Lord. Even if you might not feel particularly in need of fellowship or companionship on a given week, there are others who are lonelier than you and who are desperate for the gift of your presence. We harm our fellow church members when we absent ourselves from the public gathering of God's people, as we are unable to fulfill our mandate to build them up.[4]

We can, of course, acknowledge the blessings that livestreaming provides for those who are homebound. My congregation has a number of members who, due either to age or to sickness, cannot attend worship regularly, and they're grateful for the ability to tune in online. But I still make it a priority in my pastoral ministry to visit with them regularly face-to-face, not just through video chat or phone calls. We all know this innately: there is something powerful about personal presence. It's better to be at the stadium than to watch from home. It's better to spend a day with your friend than to simply email them. Being there matters. Let's not trick ourselves into thinking that this applies to everything except for the church.

Expect Great Things!

While showing up to worship is vital, it should never be a mechanical exercise. We should show up with great expectations of what the day in God's house will hold for us (see Pss. 63:1–4; 84:10). You should be on the edge of your seat in worship! Come with expectation and anticipation for this reason alone: you are coming to the God who does all things well. He is the God who does far more abundantly than we can ask or imagine (see Eph. 3:20).

Expect amazing things to come from even a seemingly ordinary and simple worship service—because you are meeting with an extraordinary and awesome God who speaks to us and meets all our needs through his Word. Coming to church faithfully means coming not just regularly but also full of faith! If we had such faith that God will do wonderful things in worship, we would never miss an opportunity to be in God's house. Church members are those who commit to showing up and soaking in the goodness of God's Word.

Leaning In

Not content to simply show up, church members must also seek opportunities to use their God-given gifts to bless God's people. So, a second responsibility of membership is *leaning in*, personally investing in the church not only with our time and money (see 1 Cor. 16:2) but also with our talents. There are spiritual gifts that each Christian is endowed with by the Holy Spirit (see 1 Cor. 12:4–7). Church members are called to faithfully exercise their gifts to help ensure that the church is "working properly" (Eph. 4:16).

Do you know what your spiritual gifts are? Do you recognize the ways in which you are particularly skilled to help others and encourage them? The Bible has a number of passages that list the various gifts given by the Holy Spirit. You can find them in Romans 12:3–8, 1 Corinthians 12:8–10 and 28, and 1 Peter 4:10–11—and these lists are not exhaustive. Some gifts are more public (like teaching or leadership), while others are used behind the scenes (like helping). The important thing to keep in mind is that these gifts are given by God, empowered by God, and designed to be used for God. Craig Troxel wisely writes, "Every command that Christ gives his church to practice Christian community requires the sustaining grace that he alone can supply. As fellow believers seek to welcome, encourage, comfort, admonish, serve, forbear with, build up, pray for, and speak the truth to one another, they are in constant need of his strength."[5]

If you feel stumped about the ways in which you might be gifted by the Holy Spirit, ask a trusted Christian friend or your pastor if you have one. Discerning your particular gifts is important but not worth agonizing over. Tom Schreiner says, "If you aren't sure what your spiritual gifts are, I wouldn't worry about it. If you give yourself to other believers in the church, you will inevitably be using your gifts."[6] To that end, let's consider three takeaways regarding spiritual gifts from Paul's teaching in 1 Corinthians 12.

It's Not All about You

"For the body does not consist of one member but of many" (v. 14; see also Rom. 12:3). It's not about you, Paul says! I wonder how many of the problems that local congregations face would be remedied if the members and officers and pastors would stop and realize that the church does not revolve around them. The church *is* about one person, but that person is Jesus. Further, now that he has ascended into glory, he has determined to manifest himself to the world through a plurality of people—not just you and not just me. A proper, God-glorifying use of our gifts is for "building up the church" (1 Cor. 14:12), not for building our own platform. Use your gifts to help others, not to highlight yourself.

You Really Do Matter

While it's not all about the individual, the individual still matters—*you* matter! Paul next speaks to those who might feel discouraged or displaced by the fact that they may not bring as much to the ecclesiastical table as others.

> If the foot should say, "Because I am not a hand, I do not belong to the body," that would not make it any less a part of the body. And if the ear should say, "Because I am not an eye, I do not belong to the body," that would not make it any less a part of the body. If the whole body were an eye, where would be the sense of hearing? If the whole body were an ear, where would be the sense of smell? But as it is, God arranged the members in the body, each one of them, as he chose. If all were a single member, where would the body be? As it is, there are many parts, yet one body. (1 Cor. 12:15–20)

No gift is unnecessary in Christ's church. *He* gives the gifts, after all, and he doesn't make mistakes. Calvin writes,

"The saints are gathered into the society of Christ on the principle that whatever benefits God confers upon them, they should in turn share with one another."[7]

If you think you have no way to contribute to the local church, instead recognize that, without you, the body cannot fire on all cylinders!

I have often been pleasantly surprised and humbled to discover the number of people who serve our church in silent ways that I never considered. Like when I learned that Mary came every Saturday morning to prepare the coffee for the Lord's Day. I suppose I thought the coffee just appeared on its own. I thought the same thing about the supplies in the kitchen and bathrooms, too, until I discovered Jen volunteered her time every month to make sure the church was stocked. And Marilyn! She transformed the landscape of our campus by devoting hours every week to planting, pruning, and watering the flowers. Before she came to our church, no one had the skill or time, and the garden was in need of attention (to put it lightly). Soon after her arrival, neighbors started commenting on the lovely transformation.

Or where would our church be without Dave? Our congregation had just moved into a substantially larger facility (from a 5,000-square-foot building to one that is over 25,000 square feet!). This required a new building-care committee and, more desperately, someone to chair it. The demand on this individual would be high, as the new space needed a lot of TLC and I was (understandably) turned down by the first few people I asked. When I called Dave, his answer almost made me cry: "I was praying you would call and ask me." From Dave's perspective, this wasn't a burden at all. This was exactly the kind of work he was gifted at doing, and to serve the church in this way was a blessing to him.

We Are All in This Together

Combining the previous two points, we conclude that the church can function properly only when we as its people function together. In *The Muppets*, the gang pulls off a corny gag (they call it Muppet Man) in which they try to sneak into a building by climbing into a trench coat and pretending to be a full-size adult human. Fozzie is the head and the left arm, Kermit is the stomach, Gonzo is the left leg, and so on. Shenanigans ensue, as you can imagine, and of course it doesn't work. They are not coordinated, and the "body" crumples to pieces. They all were going their own way, so their collapse was inevitable. We can learn a lesson here: as a church, we need the collaborative spirit and determination without which we will crumple to the ground like the ill-advised Muppet Man.

We do this by recognizing that every member matters. In theater, the saying goes that "there are no small parts" —the same is true in the church. No one is dispensable.

> The eye cannot say to the hand, "I have no need of you," nor again the head to the feet, "I have no need of you." On the contrary, the parts of the body that seem to be weaker are indispensable. (1 Cor. 12:21–22)

We live out that reality by avoiding cliques within the church, by prizing the abilities of others (even if—especially if—they are far different from our own), and by striving to make every member of the church feel at home.

Standing Down

If you haven't picked up on it yet, church membership requires a lot of humility! Our responsibilities include attending worship and fellowship and participating in the life of the congregation through acts of service—but one can do all of that with an air of superiority or self-ishness. This is why I say that a third responsibility of church membership, beyond showing up and leaning in, is actually *standing down*—we stand down to our own wants, preferences, and even rights. This accords with the call of the Christian in general (see Matt. 16:24), and it's essential to the peace of the church in particular (see Ps. 122:6). Church members do this as they esteem their fellow members more highly than themselves and as they submit in the Lord to their church leaders.

Esteeming Others Highly

Consider that the Bible gives over fifty instructions for how we are to live in a Christian community (the "one another" commands), and a majority of these have to do with a call to pursue that which makes for unity and peace. As John Owen observes, "There is no other Christian duty urged with more earnestness and vehemence than that of unity."[8] Here are a few representative examples:

Live in harmony with one another. (Rom. 12:16)

May the God of endurance and encouragement grant you to live in such harmony with one another, in accord with Christ Jesus, that together you may with one voice glorify the God and Father of our Lord Jesus Christ. (Rom. 15:5–6)

Aim for restoration, comfort one another, agree with one another, live in peace. (2 Cor. 13:11)

Therefore encourage one another and build one another up. (1 Thess. 5:11)

Do not grumble against one another. (James 5:9)

These are imperatives *for us.* It is easy to read passages like these and think of the responsibility that others have toward us, all while neglecting the responsibility that we have toward others! We want peace in our churches, but we rarely consider that we may be the ones hindering it. Richard Sibbes captures what must be the proper attitude of church members when he writes, "It would be a good contest amongst Christians, one to labour to give no offense, and the other to labour to take none."[9]

Many people leave a congregation when they don't get their way. They storm out when people don't see eye to eye with them on some issue, or perhaps they make life so miserable for someone in the church that they essentially force *them* to leave. Such petty behavior is not consistent with the call of the Christian community. Members of the church are to submit to one another, forgive one another, be tenderhearted to one another, comfort one another, bear with one another, encourage one another, love one another earnestly, and serve one another (see Gal. 5:13; Eph. 4:2, 32; 5:21; Col. 3:13; 1 Peter 4:8).

The New Testament repeatedly ties these commands back to Christ's role as head of the church. For example, Paul tells the Ephesians to submit "to one another out of reverence *for Christ*" (Eph. 5:21). What we often forget is that the issue we need to agree on is the lordship of Christ. He is what unites us, not our preferences or positions. When my tastes are not championed by others in the congregation, it's not a threat to my belonging in the church. What makes me a part of the church is the same thing that makes anyone else a part of it: knowing Christ and being drawn by his Spirit.

Here's the point: believers' spiritual union in Christ will produce a practical and felt unity in fellowship and community. Unity is not something that can be artificially constructed—but it doesn't have to be! Christians who have the Holy Spirit in their hearts and who have Christ as their Head are more unified than any other group on earth. In fact, they share a bond even closer than blood.

A Christian shares more in common with their fellow church member than with an unbelieving sibling. The church must hold on to this astounding truth in the face of threats to her unity. Without this theological foundation, she stands no chance of maintaining peace amid a variety of differences and disagreements.

Obeying Leaders Submissively

The Scriptures call believers to submit to the leaders whom God has placed over them in the church. "Obey your leaders and submit to them, for they are keeping watch over your souls, as those who will have to give an account. Let them do this with joy and not with groaning, for that would be of no advantage to you" (Heb. 13:17; see also 1 Peter 5:5). Following this command, some congregations require prospective members to publicly vow submission to their elders in order to join the church. In my denomination, new members must agree to "submit in the Lord to [the church's] government, and to heed its discipline, even in case you should be found delinquent in doctrine or life."[10]

The faithful church member comes with great humility, then, ready to submit to his or her leaders, not to go toe to toe with them. While the aforementioned vow noted submission in the event of doctrinal error or misconduct, it actually applies more broadly than cases of official discipline within the church. In fact, submission is required each Sunday in the worship service. How so? Every time a minister of God's Word gets into the pulpit to preach, the individual in the pew has the chance either to submit by receiving "the truth with faith, love, meekness, and readiness of mind, as the Word of God"[11] *or* to sit there and internally debate the points made by the preacher (content) or degrade the way the points are made (style). Pastor William Boekestein gets to the heart of the matter: "When you come to the sermon asking, 'How will the preacher fail today?' you'll be looking for shortcomings (Luke 11:54) rather than panning for gold. We should examine what we hear (Acts 17:11) but not with a fault-finding ear."[12]

Pastors know all too well those church members who seem to thrive off registering complaints or engaging in disputes with the leadership. That flies in the face of what membership is meant to promote, namely the peace and unity of the church. Furthermore, as we stated in chapter 1, church membership is fundamentally about how we relate to God and how he relates to us. We would do well to remember that "God opposes the proud but gives grace to the humble" (James 4:6).

So refuse to be a critic, a cynic, a warmonger, or a know-it-all. Stand down for the sake of the church and your own soul, clinging to these words: "If possible, so far as it depends on you, live peaceably with all" (Rom. 12:18).

Reaching Out

A new church member must never be content to be a church's last member. Therefore, a final responsibility of membership in a local church is *reaching out* into the surrounding community to bring other lost sheep into the safety of Christ's fold, the church.

A Great Commission

Witness and evangelism are part and parcel of belonging to a church, as we learn from Jesus's Great Commission:

> Go therefore and make disciples of all nations, baptizing them in the name of the Father and of the Son and of the Holy Spirit, teaching them to observe all that I have commanded you. And behold, I am with you always, to the end of the age. (Matt. 28:19–20)

I believe we often hear these words and divorce them from their fulfillment within the church. What Jesus is commanding here is not simply for us to get conversions. Baptism is mentioned, which, as we have already seen in previous chapters, is the initiation into the visible church. It was never meant to exist apart from the church, such that Jesus is essentially saying, "Go therefore and make disciples of all nations, bringing them into the church." Further solidifying this view is the next step commanded by Christ: "*teaching them to observe all that I have commanded you.*" That's certainly not something that can occur in a single conversation. It entails frequent, consistent, in-depth instruction in God's Word—like the kind you get in the weekly pulpit ministry of a church. Moreover, whose responsibility is it to ensure that believers "observe" the commandments of Christ and put them into practice but the elders of a local church (see 1 Peter 5:2–3)?

The Great Commission finds its fulfillment not in conversion but in the church. This means that the church member who takes the call of witness and evangelism seriously recognizes that we want more than just a "decision for Christ"—we want a disciple of Christ. Conversions are critical, and we praise God that by his Spirit he enables us to help bring them about. But that same Spirit also empowers us to bring new converts into the care of the church and walk alongside them as they grow in their faith. This is what the Great Commission is all about.

An Alluring Holiness

Beyond apologetic or evangelistic conversations with the lost, the Bible clearly teaches that another important way in which people are drawn to church is through her holiness. That is to say, when the church behaves like the church, she is different from the world, and this difference is *attractive*.

Peter writes, "Keep your conduct among the Gentiles honorable, so that when they speak against you as evildoers, they may see your good deeds and glorify God on the day of visitation" (1 Peter 2:12). The word *honorable* could also be translated as "beautiful" or "attractive." There should be an attractiveness in a believer's lifestyle, an allure that can counter and conquer the allure of sin in the world, so that those who do not know Christ would see him in us and would rather have what we have than have the sin that is calling their name. Do you have an *attractive* lifestyle? I'm not talking about a lifestyle that makes someone drool with envy, but one that makes their heart beat with a fundamental longing. Instagram is for the former; the church is for the latter.

A congregant of mine once had to fight for his life over the course of several weeks in the hospital. Doug was battling a severe illness, and it seemed to be winning. By God's grace, his life was spared. At one point, after finally returning home, Doug told me that a number of nurses and doctors commented on how much they appreciated caring for him. In fact, one nurse was asked to work overtime, and she said that she would only do it if she were assigned to Doug. Another would stop by Doug's room after every single shift, sit on his bed, thank him, and assure him that everything would be okay. She didn't need to do that, but she wanted to be with him. Now, I don't need to tell you that there's nothing attractive about standing at death's door—and yet these people were drawn to Doug. Why? I asked Doug, and he said, "They said it was because I didn't complain. I just kept telling them how much I appreciated what they did for me." *Keep your conduct attractive among the Gentiles.* I replied, "Doug, you were showing them Christ. You were witnessing. They were seeing the Savior in you!" It wasn't evangelism that made the difference—it was just his lifestyle.

This makes me think of a letter that nineteenth-century Scottish minister Robert Murray M'Cheyne once received regarding his preaching. Someone had visited his church recently and wrote, "I heard you preach last Sabbath evening, and it pleased God to bless that sermon to my soul. It was not so much what you said, as your manner of speaking that struck me. I saw in you a beauty in holiness that I never saw before."[13]

This, then, is one of the most important—albeit most difficult—responsibilities of the church member: to live a life that looks like Christ's. We are to die to sin and live to righteousness, "to walk in a manner worthy of the Lord, fully pleasing to him: bearing fruit in every good work" (Col. 1:10; see also Phil. 1:27). We must "renounce ungodliness and worldly passions, and to live self-controlled, upright, and godly lives in the present age" (Titus 2:12). It's hard work, but God uses it to draw others to himself, because something remarkable happens when we pursue holiness: the image of our Maker is made clearer, brighter, more conspicuous in us—and people are drawn to *him*. As Jesus taught in the Sermon on the Mount, when we as the church live out our identity as "the light of the world," others will "see [our] good works and give glory to [our] Father who is in heaven" (Matt. 5:14, 16).

Members of God's church sever their allegiance with sin to make a better one with Jesus. They commit to sanctification and pursue purity, adding to—not detracting from—the alluring splendor of the body of Christ. Members of the church recognize that their responsibility is not simply to worship the Lord but to do so *"in the beauty of holiness"* (Ps. 29:2 KJV).

Conclusion

After this survey of the expectations and responsibilities of church membership, you would be forgiven if your initial response was "No thank you! Not for me!" The church requires our time, talents, humility, and holiness. None of these is an easy ask. Here is where we must remember that Christ never calls us to anything that he himself has not experienced for us. He lived a life devoted to the fullhearted worship of his Father, with all the religious responsibilities that it entailed. From an early age, he made his priorities known—"Did you not know that I must be in my Father's house?" (Luke 2:49)—and he was consumed with a holy jealousy for God's worship (see John 2:17). His life and ministry were impeccable, and he resisted the pull of sin (Matt. 4). Further, he "came not to be served but to serve" (Mark 10:45), humbling himself all the way to death on the cross (Phil. 2:8).

Everything that Christ asks of us in the church he has already done for us in the gospel. That's a paradigm-shifting reality that we all need to hold on to. When the gospel invades our thinking about all of life—not just how we are saved but also how we serve—it is transformative. What I would otherwise approach with drudgery and disdain I can now approach with delight. And since I'm still a sinner, there's still drudgery from time to time. But when the love of Christ fills my heart, it overflows such that the only proper response is for me to love him in return—not just because we are *commanded* to do it but because we feel really and truly *compelled* to do it. We can say, with Newton, that duty and pleasure are bound up together!

> It is our highest pleasure,
> No less than duty's call;
> To love him beyond measure,
> And serve him with our all.[14]

Do you see the gospel blessings that fuel our obedience? Do you see the motivation? It's as simple as this, really: Christ gave his life for you, so you can give your life to his church.

Questions for Further Discussion

1. Of the responsibilities of church membership listed in this chapter, which do you find to be the most challenging, and why?
2. Why is attending worship faithfully so important?
3. What are some of the challenges and rewards you experience when using your specific gifts within the church?

4. In what ways does church membership require humility?

5. In what ways is our membership tied to the Great Commission? How might you fulfill your calling to be a witness to those outside the church this week?

QUESTIONS AND ANSWERS
ON CHURCH MEMBERSHIP

Church membership is nothing if not practical, and the subject raises a lot of important questions. I have certainly not listed all those questions here (I had stopped at a nice round number, but then my editor made me add one more question—so twenty-six it is!), nor have I fully answered the ones that I did include. Nonetheless, I hope you will find the following to be a helpful guide through some of the pricklier practicalities of membership in a local body of Christ's church.

How can I know which church I should join?

There are likely a number of churches in your town (there are literally hundreds in mine!). So which one should you join? Assuming that the options before you all bear the marks of a true church (the preaching of God's Word, the pure administration of the sacraments, and the exercise of church discipline; see chapter 1), you may be helped in your search by considering the following three questions (bathing them all in much prayer, of course!).

First, *where can you worship God well?* Certain worship styles or practices may not align with your personal convictions. Perhaps a church holds to a certain doctrinal distinctive that you disagree with and that you will not be able to overlook. If you feel that you cannot participate wholeheartedly in Lord's Day worship, because you will be either distracted or discouraged, you should probably not join that congregation. Look for a church where you can freely offer up a sacrifice of praise week in and week out.

Second, *where can you use your gifts and be of the most service?* There may be a number of good churches that you enjoy; however, not all will be in equal need of your particular gifting. For example, let's say that you are a talented musician. All else being equal, the local church plant in need of someone to help lead congregational singing might be a better place for you to join than the other church across town with a robust music ministry. Look for a church where you can maximally use your gifts and abilities.

Third, *where will you be spiritually nourished the most?* There may be a number of churches in your area with solid biblical teaching, as well as opportunities for service, but you might find that you are challenged and edified by the preaching of one over the other. This should be given serious weight in your evaluation. Here are some other things to look for: Will the members of the congregation serve as examples of godliness, pushing you to grow in your sanctification and flourish in your faith? Will you be sharpened and honed through the ministries of this church? Will you find opportunities for fellowship and people with whom you can go through the ups and downs of life? That is a good church indeed.

Note well, though, that the sequence of these questions matters. If we reverse the order, we can err by making our church selection just like any other consumeristic decision: What's in it for *me*? Our needs are important, to be sure, but they are not the most important. As in the rest of the Christian life, God and neighbor come before self. I believe if you find a church where you can worship God well and serve others meaningfully, you will have also found a church that will build you up and feed your soul—and having found that church, join it!

Do I need to join the church that is nearest to me?

No, there is no biblical mandate that says you must attend the church closest to you—though there can be wisdom in doing so. When it comes to serving the body and being built up through its fellowship, proximity does matter. If you're thinking of joining a church that's a bit of a hike from your home, check two things. First, check your *motivation*: Why *not* join the church closest to you? This wasn't even a question before the invention of the automobile. It wasn't long ago that churchgoers had no choice but to worship at the church in their local parish. But now, with just a little driving, we can avoid relational difficulties, escape church discipline, or give into whatever consumeristic impulse is catching our fancy. Do you have a good reason for commuting?

Second, check your *willingness*: Can you commit to the responsibilities of membership in this particular congregation, even with the added burdens of time in the car and cash at the pump? Do you have kids? Will they be able to handle the constraints of commuting, or of living far away from new friends they might make? It can certainly be done. Some of the most devoted members I have served and worshipped with have made the longest hauls—faithfully attending morning and evening worship, Wednesday prayer meeting, and all kinds of other activities within the church. To those who lived a lot closer but who made less of an effort and less of an appearance, the commitment of those who lived farther away was an inspiration to make church a priority.

There is no good church where I am moving—what should I do?

You should consider not moving there. Seriously. When we contemplate making a big move, often for work, we will do a lot of research and evaluation before we actually pull the trigger. We will hire people to help us find a good home, we will ensure that the schooling options are acceptable, we will see if there's a good gym nearby, we will check for our favorite stores. Church is often an afterthought, when it should really be the first thing we take into consideration—after all, the effects of church life reach into the next life, unlike those of any other endeavor. I was encouraged by a recent phone call in which a young man who was considering moving to the area wanted to learn more about our church to see if it would be a good fit for him and his wife. The most impressive part? They weren't moving for over a year! He was looking for a church before even looking for a house.

Now, if such a move is outside of your control, then see the two questions answered above. You could join the best option close by: the place where you can best worship, best serve, and be best fed, even if one or all of those is not ideal. Or, alternatively, you could commit to making a lengthy commute in order to attend a church that checks those boxes for you. You should also pray that the Lord would plant a solid congregation in your new place of residence, and you should do what you can to help make that happen.

Should I join a church (or transfer my membership) if I'm moving away temporarily (for example, for college or a transient work situation)?

This is a decision that should be made in consultation with the leadership at both churches. See how they would advise you to handle the temporary relocation. The important thing is that you have elders who will look out for you and check in on you. Spiritual oversight is critical at all times in the Christian life, perhaps especially when we are away from our home base and when the temptations to sin can feel more intense.

Will I need to share my testimony in order to join a church?

Yes, somewhere along the process of becoming a member of a church, you will need to share your testimony. Since the visible church is made up of those who profess the true religion, the leaders of the church—who are charged with admitting or excluding members—will need to hear that true profession. Churches will do this in a variety of ways. Perhaps you will be asked to share the story of how you came to saving faith in a private meeting with the elders and pastors, or you might be asked to do so publicly before the church, in written or spoken form. If that seems daunting, don't let it be a reason you run from membership. Our story of salvation should always be on our lips. Jesus said,

> So everyone who acknowledges me before men, I also will acknowledge before my Father who is in heaven, but whoever denies me before men, I also will deny before my Father who is in heaven. (Matt. 10:32–33)

The church I want to join is requiring me to make "vows" for membership—isn't that a bit extreme?

Jesus teaches, "Let what you say be simply 'Yes' or 'No'; anything more than this comes from evil" (Matt. 5:37), but this is not a prohibition on ever swearing an oath or making a vow (Paul does this himself in several places, such as Romans 1:9). Rather, it is a denunciation of invoking God's name in petty promises. On serious occasions, it is quite appropriate to call upon God as a means of underscoring our commitment to keep a promise. The fact that some bristle at the thought of making public vows for church membership is perhaps an indication of our society's low view of the church. We want to be able to cancel at any time, like we can with our magazine subscriptions. While they do not bind us to one congregation "till death do us part," membership vows make us think more carefully about the responsibilities of church membership, spurring us to greater fidelity to Christ and his people (see Pss. 50:14; 76:11). They are most appropriate.

Do I need to take a new members class to join a church? What if I have already done so at a previous church that holds to the same doctrines?

The onboarding process of membership will vary from church to church, but it is not uncommon for congregations to require new members to attend some sort of class or small group that will introduce them to the distinctives of that particular congregation. Sometimes this can feel like a chore, especially if we assume that we are not going to learn anything new in the class (for example, you may be transferring your membership from a Presbyterian church in one state to a Presbyterian church in another state). I would encourage you not to bemoan the process, though. For one thing, the class affords a great opportunity to get to know other potential members of the church, and especially the leaders. It is also a crucial first step of submitting to the leadership of the church and humbly acknowledging their authority in your life, which will be a requirement throughout the duration of your membership. Finally, we can never study the subject of God's gospel, his Word, or his church too much!

Do I need to get rebaptized to join a church?

Perhaps you were baptized before you were converted, or at a Christian summer camp when you were a kid, or in a different denomination from the one you are about to join. It's not uncommon to then wonder, "Did that count? Do I need to do it again?" No, you don't need to do it again—as long as you received a valid Christian baptism.

Now the question becomes, what makes for a valid baptism? Two things: water and the Word. Water is to be administered to the person being baptized, "in the name of the Father and of the Son and of the Holy Spirit" (Matt. 28:19—that's "the Word" part). This act visibly identifies a person with Christ's death and resurrection. So if that took place, you should not be "rebaptized." Baptism should only be administered once, since our regeneration and union with Christ is a once-for-all event.

The Presbyterian and Reformed tradition has held that it is God's work that makes a baptism efficacious, not the church the baptism takes place in, the person who administers it, or the manner in which the person being baptized gets wet. The Westminster Confession says that "the grace which is exhibited in or by the sacraments rightly used, is not conferred by any power in them; neither doth the efficacy of a sacrament depend upon the piety or intention of him that doth administer it: but upon the work of the Spirit, and the word of institution."[1] Baptism is not about the person or the church that administers it. It's about God and his promises to us, which are unbreakable and unchangeable, and which never need a "redo."

Presbyterians sometimes talk about "noncommunicant" members—what is that?

Presbyterian and Reformed churches make the distinction between *noncommunicant* members and *communicant* members, or sometimes between *baptized* members and *professing* members. Both are members, but baptized members are so by virtue of the profession of their parent(s), while professing members are so by virtue of their own profession. To be clear, we are not saying that these children are saved just because they are in the church. But the covenantal nature of God's dealing with his people means that the privileges of the church are theirs to lose.

The term "noncommunicant" finds its meaning in relation to the sacrament of Communion. Those who are members of the church by baptism but who have yet to profess their personal faith in Jesus are not permitted to come to the Lord's Table. To some, that might sound absurd. How can Presbyterians claim someone is a Christian but then withhold a critical component of Christian nurture and growth from them? But we're actually *not* saying that. Again, we do not equate membership with conversion. The church "consists of all those throughout the world that profess the true religion; *and of their children*"[2]—even if those children have not yet professed faith. So, while the children of believers are considered members of the church, certain privileges of that membership are withheld until they demonstrate and profess a personal faith in the Lord, which is required in order to come worthily to the Lord's Supper (see 1 Cor. 11:28–29). By way of comparison, consider some of the age restrictions in the United States: an eight-year-old and an eighteen-year-old are both citizens, but the former is not permitted to drive or vote, while the latter is. Certain privileges are withheld until a person is of age, without calling into question the reality that they belong. The same is true of baptized infants and children in the church.[3]

Is there a particular age at which a noncommunicant member should make a profession of faith?

No. Certainly a child has to be old enough to "discern the difference between the Lord's Table and snack time,"[4] but beyond that, churches should not expect their children to profess faith at an arbitrary age, say twelve or eighteen. This is because a child might be ready before twelve or not ready at eighteen. A profession of faith must be exactly that. It's not reading a script or conforming to the expectations of one's parents or parish. It's an expression of a genuine trust in Jesus Christ. Thus, children should not be admitted into communicant membership until the church leadership is convinced that they have a personal, saving knowledge of him. For some people, that comes early; for others, it doesn't come until well into adulthood.

Do I need to give financially to my church?

In the old covenant, giving was mandated in order to support the worship of God, particularly as a means of compensating the Levitical priests (see Num. 18:21–24). In a similar fashion, the church today survives off the financial gifts of her members. If membership requires our service and commitment, it's hard to imagine how that would not include our money too. Paul includes this responsibility of membership in his instructions to the Corinthians: "On the first day of every week, *each of you* is to put something aside and store it up" (1 Cor. 16:2).

But we should not view our financial gifts merely as dues owed for services rendered. Rather, giving is an act freighted with spiritual significance. Scripture is clear that what we do with our money speaks volumes about what we love with our hearts. Jesus taught, "For where your treasure is, there your heart will be also" (Matt. 6:21; see also Heb. 13:5). For Christians, should our hearts not be with the church? Furthermore, our financial offerings are one of the most tangible ways we can support our brothers and sisters in the Lord, which is the primary context for the discussions of giving in the New

Testament (see Rom. 12:13; 15:24; 1 Cor. 16:1; 2 Cor. 8:1–7; Phil. 4:14–18).

How much money am I expected to give to the church?

Unlike in the old covenant, there is no explicit command in the new covenant to "tithe," or to give ten percent. Rather, when we turn the page to the New Testament, we see that the focus shifts from *how much* we must give to *how* we must give. That is the better question. To answer it, we could highlight a few principles of giving. First, we should give *as an act of cheerfulness*: "Each one must give as he has decided in his heart, not reluctantly or under compulsion, for God loves a cheerful giver" (2 Cor. 9:7). The word translated as "cheerful" is the Greek *hilaros*, meaning "merry," from which we get our word "hilarious." Derek Thomas explains, "God loves it when His children are overflowing in happiness in their giving. As a parent is overjoyed when a son or daughter makes something and presents it as a gift, even if the gift (in itself) is nothing much to speak about. The joy in giving stems from a heart that is filled with gospel grace. 'It is more blessed to give than to receive' (Acts 20:35)."[5]

Second, we should give *as an act of service to others*. When we view our money as something that can be used by God to bless others, we will actually be eager and excited to give it away. That was what Paul noticed about the churches in Macedonia: "They gave according to their means, as I can testify, and beyond their means, of their own accord, begging us earnestly for the favor of taking part in the relief of the saints" (2 Cor. 8:3–4). Here you find an impoverished church that is seeking an opportunity to give above and beyond its means to bless others in affliction. What would lead it to do such a thing? The only answer is the great riches it had received through Jesus Christ.

Third, we should give *as an act of thanksgiving for the gospel*. Paul roots the imperative for giving in the indicative of the incarnation, ministry, and death of Christ: "For you know the grace of our Lord Jesus Christ, that though he was rich, yet for your sake he became poor, so that you by his poverty might become rich" (2 Cor. 8:9). When we think about the subject of giving, we must remind ourselves that we are indeed "rich" in Christ. In him, we have "all things" (Rom. 8:32; see also 1 Cor 3:21; Eph. 1:3)! When we give, we reflect our Savior, who did not hold on to his riches but gave them to us (see Phil. 2:4–10). His sacrifice should inspire ours, meager though it will be in comparison. With all of this in mind, we see that there might be a reason the New Testament doesn't stipulate how much of our income should go to the church. After all, could you possibly put a value on the gift of salvation? The proper response to the cross is not a portion of my bank account, but the entirety of my being. As Isaac Watts put it, "Love so amazing, so divine, demands my soul, my life, my all."[6] We shouldn't be content with a mere percentage—rather, like the Macedonians, we should be eager to give above and beyond our means for the glory of Christ.

There are so many different churches and denominations. Isn't the whole point of Christianity to get along with everyone?

The Bible certainly has a lot to say about the importance of Christian unity (see Ps. 133:1; Eph. 4:3; Phil. 2:2; Col. 3:14). It would be wonderful if every believer could live, serve, and worship with one another. And we will one day—in glory. In that respect, the reality of denominationalism is a *sad* thing—but I don't think it's a *bad* thing. Put another way, although denominations would not exist in a sinless world, they are not sinful in and of themselves. The Bible even shows that, sometimes, for the sake of the mission of the gospel, it's better for people to part ways (see Acts 15:36–41).

Surprising as it may seem, denominations can actually help us fulfill our calling to love one another, serve Christ, and even dwell in unity! How so? Picture two groups of believers: they're part of the same church, yet each one has strongly held convictions that differ from those of the other. Worship would be a distraction, and service and missions would likely be derailed by constant infighting. But when those believers belong to different denominations that align with their respective convictions, they can now worship freely and stay focused on their various callings. Moreover, with these doctrinal distinctives no longer distracting anyone, these groups of Christians can actually enjoy the unity that they have in Christ. Denominations, when properly understood and when properly functioning, do not threaten Christian unity—they actually help preserve and promote it.

Isn't membership elitist? Jesus welcomes everyone!

Membership is not elitist, though I'm sure that it can be twisted by some in the church to make it seem that way. Those in the church are not better than those outside it, though they are distinct from them. In the Christian faith, there is an interesting blend of both inclusivity and exclusivity. While it's true that Jesus welcomes everyone (see "Come to me, all who labor and are heavy laden"— Matt. 11:28), he still clearly distinguishes between those who have taken up that offer and those who have not (see "Whoever believes in the Son has eternal life; whoever does not obey the Son shall not see life, but the wrath of God remains on him"—John 3:36). The purpose of church membership is not to assert the members' superiority to others, but rather to assert their association with the Savior —an association that is open to all who believe!

If I'm a member, do I need to attend every function that my church hosts? Which ones should I prioritize?

No, it would be quite unreasonable to assume that churchgoers can actually attend every single thing the church hosts. We have to make decisions about our time, our emotional bandwidth, and all the rest. Is there any biblical direction as to what church events we should prioritize? The apostolic church gives us a great answer to this question: "They devoted themselves to the apostles' teaching and the fellowship, to the breaking of bread and the prayers" (Acts 2:42). This verse lists four things that church members were devoted to: preaching, prayer, the sacraments, and fellowship with one another. These four should be our holy "addictions," too, and the easiest way to ensure that we get all of them is by prioritizing Lord's Day worship. Beyond that, fill your calendar as much as possible with opportunities to open the Bible with fellow church members, time to pray with God's people (go to the prayer meeting!), and other sweet moments of fellowship. These will all be good for your soul.

I think a good point to get down is this: what happens in the church shouldn't be an afterthought. It shouldn't be something you squeeze in. The church member should, as much as possible, try to sync the rhythms of their own life with the rhythms of church life. We show up to church because we have a ministry to others. Hebrews exhorts us to "stir up one another to love and good works" (10:24). We can't do that if we're not with others. When I see a couple whom I know has had to struggle to get to church, I'm encouraged in my own obedience. Hopefully, my presence does the same for someone else. God can use our participation in church to stimulate other saints toward their true purpose.

The spiritual gift of "being there" is one that almost anyone can have but that few exercise.[7] Take it from a pastor: it means *so much* when people simply show up to functions of the church. You don't need to come early and set up or stay late and tear down (though that wouldn't hurt!), and you don't need to lead a lesson or offer a prayer (though that would be welcome too!)—just being there means more than you might think.

How can I support and encourage my pastor?

Pray for him and his family. Take an interest in his wife and kids, and be kind and compassionate to them. Listen attentively to his sermons. Give due weight to his advice when it's offered. Take a moment to text him or call him and simply say, "Thank you." Oh, and like I said above, show up as often as you can to church events and just be there!

I disagree with my pastor or elders on an issue. What should I do?

You should feel free to share that disagreement with your leadership, albeit in a respectful manner. Godly leaders are to be humble leaders, and there should be an openness and a graciousness on their part in hearing a congregant's differing views. Leaders are not infallible, and perhaps they have erred on a particular issue. However, you should also prepare for the possibility that you are wrong in this disagreement and that God is graciously using the leadership in your church to reveal that to you.

When addressing differences with others in the church, whether the leadership or the laity, you must always seek to

> walk in a manner worthy of the calling to which you
> have been called, with all humility and gentleness, with
> patience, bearing with one another in love, eager to
> maintain the unity of the Spirit in the bond of peace.
> (Eph. 4:1–3)

How should I respond when my pastor points out sin in my life?

It's one of the frustrating ironies of pastoral ministry that a primary responsibility of the pastor—namely, to address sin in his congregants' lives (see 1 Tim. 5:20; Titus 2:15; 3:10–11)—is what makes congregants most upset! Charles Spurgeon has a wonderfully instructive word for us on this count:

> Surely, we do not wish to be left in a fool's paradise,
> pleased with the idea that we are rich and increased in
> goods, and have need of nothing, when all the while
> we are naked, and poor, and miserable. We desire to be
> informed as to our own condition. . . . Dear friend, for
> this reason do not be angry with the minister if, when
> you go to hear him on the Lord's-day, his text is not a
> promise, or a sweet bit of doctrine, but a warning, and
> an exhortation, or a condemnation. . . . It may be the
> very thing you need. If God has sent you a bitter potion,

it will be better for you than the sweetest dainties the smooth-tongued flatterer could prepare. Cry to God to search you, and to make you to know your true condition as before his face.[8]

The pastor plays a special role in our sanctification, if we will let him. We should weigh carefully and prayerfully the reproof we receive from God's ministers.

Should I join a church that doesn't have programs for my kids?

Yes. Or rather, the lack of such programming should never be the reason why you don't join a church. That's because what your children need are not programs but the preaching of the Word of God. They need exactly what you need. This is not to say that there is no place for things like Sunday school or youth groups (as long as they do not interfere with Lord's Day worship). But if you find a church with a great youth ministry but a weak ministry of the Word, your spiritual life will suffer, and that will trickle down to affect your children.

Also, a congregation might not offer a lot for kids because they don't have a lot of kids—and you leaving won't fix that. I have often quipped that if every prospective member who didn't join our church because they wanted a youth group for their kids had actually stuck around, we would have the biggest one in the city by now.

I have been hurt by a church in the past, and I have zero interest in joining one again. What should I do?

It's a sad reality that in a fallen world, the church *will* hurt her own—whether through unintentional offense or wicked abuse. If that has been your experience, I am deeply sorry. Further, I want to say that it is an entirely understandable and natural reaction to seek to run from the sorts of people or structures that have hurt us. But Christians aren't ever allowed to write off the church. Why? A few reasons.

To begin with, the Bible never actually suggests that leaving the church entirely is an appropriate response to being hurt by the church. Paul writes to numerous churches where there are all sorts of messed-up things going on, and his advice is not to leave, but to reach into the vast well of God's grace to find the strength necessary to love, forgive, and change. He never permits real hurt and pain to excuse Christians from the responsibility of assembling together, submitting to their leaders, and serving the Lord together. Even if unresolved hurt forces us to another congregation, it must not force us out of the church completely.

It also must be said that Jesus is with his church. If you give up on the church, you're giving up on more than you realize. If anyone can heal your hurts, it is him. Stick with the church because you want to stick with Jesus. Remember that even though the church hurt him—indeed, pursued him to death—he did not give up on her! And, as paradoxical as it sounds, the church is one of the means by which Christ helps even the Christians who have been hurt by her. He gives "the shepherds and teachers . . . for building up the body of Christ" (Eph. 4:11–12).

I feel like the Holy Spirit is leading me to take a break from the church in order to heal from past hurts. Is that okay?

No. And the Holy Spirit isn't leading you that way, either. The Holy Spirit's role is to draw us into closer communion with Christ. One of the primary ways we get more of Jesus is through getting more of his Word and more of his people. The Holy Spirit draws people *to* the church—where those things are found—never away from it.

I feel disconnected at my church. What can I do to foster more meaningful relationships?

A place that is meant to foster belonging can often feel terribly lonely. This is particularly true if you feel that you do not fit in with a majority culture in the church: maybe you are single, and most are married, or you have kids, and most don't, and so on. Those sorts of differences should not separate us in the church. How can we overcome this distance?

1. Be proactive. Sometimes people tell me they feel disconnected at church, and yet they do nothing to promote connection. They leave immediately after worship, or they stand sullenly in a corner, expecting others to come and engage them. Step out first. Bless others as you wish they would bless you (see Luke 6:31). Make an effort to speak to people at church, and follow up with actual, intentional opportunities to fellowship together.

2. *Practice hospitality.* The Bible commands us to do this (see 1 Peter 4:9). One of the best ways to break down barriers between you and others at church is to get them into your home. If it seems daunting to host people who are relatively unfamiliar to you, why not invite an existing friend as well?

3. *Pray without ceasing.* We should pray for friends, and we should pray for our friends. In other words, pray that the Lord would give you good relationships in the church, and on top of that, pray for the specific people in your church. You will feel more connected to those people whom you regularly bring to God in prayer.

I struggle with mental and emotional health challenges that make it very difficult for me to be around large groups of people. What should I do about church membership?

Don't let this very real difficulty keep you from the church or from joining her. The church is a gathering of people who have all sorts of challenges. You should inform your pastor or elders of your hesitance to stick around in large gatherings, so that they understand. They can then be praying for you, and they can try to facilitate fellowship and community for you in ways that are appropriate. Also, never stop praying that the Lord would heal you and enable you to enjoy the body of believers in a fuller and freer way.

How can I know when it's time to leave my church?

Leaving a church should be done very carefully, and only after much prayer and discussion with your leadership and with any family that may be involved. It should not be a rash decision, and the legitimate reasons that can occasion separating yourself from a church are actually pretty few. In fact, beyond relocation, let me list just three.

1. Ministry faithfulness. One reason to leave a church could be that God is calling you into a new season of ministry and service somewhere else. That is, there may be absolutely nothing wrong at your current church, and yet you feel led to, say, help start a church plant in another part of town. Or maybe you feel that your gifts are needed on the mission field in another country. In order to remain faithful to God's calling on your life, it may be that you actually need to say goodbye to a church that you love dearly. Hopefully, the church you are leaving supports this vision and can send you off with their prayers and encouragement.

2. Doctrinal fidelity. If the church of which you are a member has strayed from the truth of God's Word, you not only *should* leave but *must* leave. I am speaking not of doctrinal *differences* but rather of doctrinal *error*. The church is to be the "pillar and buttress of the truth" (1 Tim. 3:15). If you cannot say that about your church, then she is no longer a church, and you need to leave.

3. Gospel focus. In another scenario, a church might be doctrinally sound, yet focused on something other than the gospel of Christ. Perhaps points of theological minutiae occupy the majority of sermons, or maybe the leadership stresses current political or social issues and cultural transformation. Here is the question you need to ask: Does your church preach nothing but Christ and him crucified? Are you reminded of your need for a Savior and of his love and mercy for you each and every week? Are you shown the multifaceted beauty of the gospel of God as his Word is opened up from the pulpit? Your soul needs that. If a church has lost its first love for Jesus (see Rev. 2:4), you should seriously consider leaving to find a church that can say, "[We] decided to know nothing among you except Jesus Christ and him crucified" (1 Cor. 2:2).

I'm hurt and upset, and I'm about to leave my church. Can you talk me off the ledge?

Don't leave for *petty reasons*. A new carpet color in the sanctuary does not threaten Christian unity or worship. A new hymnal or Bible translation in the pew rack should not cause you to leave a church.

Don't leave over *personal offenses*. Christians will sin against one another and will offend one another. That's an inevitable part of doing life with other fallen human beings. It's true in families, schools, neighborhoods, and workplaces. Anywhere sinners come together, they will inevitably offend one another. The difference in the church is that Christians overlook offenses and cover them in love (see 1 Peter 4:8). To leave a church because you have been offended is a poor witness.

Similarly, don't leave over the *presence of sin*. There is sin in every church. Let's say a leader has sinned—should you leave? Not necessarily. Abandoning the church certainly won't promote holiness. The key is to address sin, work through it, and come out the other side sanctified and more Christlike. I am not saying that we will always be successful, but we miss an opportunity for such important change if we simply pack up and leave when messiness comes to the surface.

One church scholar, Joseph Hellerman, argues that sanctification occurs especially in those believers "who stick it out through the often messy process of interpersonal discord and conflict resolution. Long-term interpersonal relationships are the crucible of genuine progress in the Christian life. People who stay also grow."[9] If you want to grow, then be ready to stay. And remember: there are always far more reasons to stay at a church than to leave it.

I have a close friend who claims they are a Christian but who has no interest in joining or even attending church. What can I do?

I am assuming that you have done a few things already: you have prayed for them, graciously challenged them, and invited them to attend church with you. None of those are onetime tries either. Keep doing them! But let me add something else that you could consider: speak often and speak well of the church. Let it be a recurring theme in your conversations. Let the blessings of your membership in the church be so abundantly evident and deeply cherished that the people of Christ become beautiful to your friend. We are made for the church, and we are made to belong to God by belonging to his people. Your joyful witness to this truth may be the very thing that draws your friend back to their true home.

RECOMMENDED RESOURCES

Introductory

Allberry, Sam. *Why Bother with Church? and Other Questions about Why You Need It and Why It Needs You.* Questions Christians Ask. Epsom, UK: The Good Book Company, 2016. [This is a wonderful introduction to give to people who don't think church matters all that much. Though it's written to cover a broad range of ecclesiastical and denominational views, it nevertheless will challenge those who see little value to participating wholeheartedly in the church.]

Cruse, Jonathan Landry. *What Happens When We Worship.* Grand Rapids: Reformation Heritage Books, 2020. [This book of mine explores the most important ministry of the church and her members: worship. It will walk you through the elements of a Reformed worship service, from call to worship to benediction, and help you gain an appreciation for the privilege the church has to meet with the Lord!]

Ferguson, Sinclair B. *Devoted to God's Church: Core Values for Christian Fellowship.* Edinburgh: Banner of Truth, 2020. [This is a splendid introduction to the nature of the church and what it means to belong to her.]

Hill, Megan. *A Place to Belong: Learning to Love the Local Church.* Wheaton, IL: Crossway, 2020. [This accessible book unravels some of the major metaphors of the church found in Scripture. Hill does a superb job of drawing out the inherent blessing of belonging to a congregation.]

McGraw, Ryan M., and Ryan Speck. *Is Church Membership Biblical?* Cultivating Biblical Godliness. Grand Rapids: Reformation Heritage Books, 2015. [This booklet covers some of the same ground we have covered here regarding the biblical rationale for church membership. It's good to hand out to visitors at church or those who are just indicating an interest in the subject.]

Intermediate

Clarkson, David. *Prizing Public Worship.* Edited by Jonathan Landry Cruse. Puritan Treasures for Today. Grand Rapids: Reformation Heritage Books, 2023. [This is a collection of three sermons from Puritan David Clarkson that talk about the responsibilities of church members in attending worship and sitting dutifully under the ministry of the preaching of God's Word.]

Clowney, Edmund P. *The Church.* Contours of Christian Theology. Downers Grove, IL: InterVarsity, 1995. [This is a systematic volume that covers the major points of ecclesiology in an academic yet accessible way.]

Kuiper, R. B. *The Glorious Body of Christ: A Scriptural Appreciation of the One Holy Church.* Reprint. London: Banner of Truth, 1967. [Though it is slightly dated, this is probably my favorite intermediate-level work of ecclesiology. The chapters are brief and to the point, yet devotional and practical in their approach. Kuiper covers a lot of ground, too—fifty-three chapters!]

Owen, John. *Duties of Christian Fellowship: A Manual for Church*

Members. Reprint. Edinburgh: Banner of Truth, 2017. [This is a very short booklet that unpacks the responsibilities of church members to their minister as well as to their fellow members. I have listed it under intermediate resources simply because it's Owen, but do know that it's the easiest work of his to read!]

Waters, Guy Prentiss. *How Jesus Runs the Church*. Phillipsburg, NJ: P&R, 2011. [For those interested in a deeper dive on matters of church polity, Waters is the best resource. Go here to understand how Presbyterianism works and why it matters.]

Advanced

Bannerman, James. *The Church of Christ*. Reprint. Edinburgh: Banner of Truth, 2014. [Bannerman was a nineteenth-century Scottish theologian. This work on ecclesiology is dense and long, yet rewarding. It covers just about everything you would need to know from a Presbyterian perspective regarding what the church is and what it means to be a member within her.]

Horton, Michael S. *People and Place: A Covenant Ecclesiology*. Louisville: Westminster John Knox Press, 2008. [This book is not for the faint of heart! Horton roots his ecclesiology within the rubric of God's covenant dealings with his people. This has massive implications for what it means to be a part of the church.]

NOTES

Foreword

1   David E. Garland, *1 Corinthians*, Baker Exegetical Commentary on the New Testament (Grand Rapids: Baker Academic, 2003), 674.

Introduction

1   Augustine, *Confessions*, 1.1.1, in *Basic Writings of Saint Augustine*, ed. Whitney J. Oates (New York: Random House, 1948), 1:3.

2   "Religion," Gallup, accessed April 29, 2024, https://news.gallup.com /poll/1690/Religion.aspx.

3   Jim Davis and Michael Graham, with Ryan P. Burge, *The Great Dechurching: Who's Leaving, Why Are They Going, and What Will It Take to Bring Them Back?*, (Grand Rapids: Zondervan, 2023), 3.

4   Robert D. Putnam, *Bowling Alone: The Collapse and Revival of American Community* (New York: Simon and Schuster, 2001).

5   John Bunyan expressed this well in his classic *The Pilgrim's Progress* when the character Ignorance (the very opposite of wisdom) says, "I take my pleasure in walking alone, even more . . . than in company." So if you want to be ignorant, you will go it alone in life. If you want to be wise, though, you will keep close company. See John Bunyan, *The Pilgrim's Progress* (1678; repr., Edinburgh: Banner of Truth, 2017), 167.

Chapter 1: The Nature of Church Membership

1   Update: We did not get there.

2   Edmund P. Clowney, *The Church*, Contours of Christian Theology (Downers Grove, IL: InterVarsity Press, 1995), 29.

3 Louis Berkhof, *Systematic Theology*, new ed. (Grand Rapids: Eerdmans, 1996), 564.

4 Westminster Confession of Faith, chapter 25.1.

5 Westminster Confession of Faith, chapter 25.2.

6 The case for infant baptism lies outside the scope of this book. But for a helpful treatment of this subject, see Jason Helopoulos's book in this series, *Covenantal Baptism*, Blessings of the Faith (Phillipsburg, NJ: P&R, 2021), 37–53.

7 Westminster Confession of Faith, chapter 28.1.

8 Helpful on this score is Harrison Perkins, *Reformed Covenant Theology: A Systematic Introduction* (Bellingham, WA: Lexham Academic, 2024), 399–406. "The sacrament of entry into God's people always signified new spiritual life but never guaranteed that its external application ensured its internal reality, as the Old Testament exhortations for those who were physically circumcised to have circumcised hearts shows. . . . This situation, where the external mark of the covenant does not necessarily grant its spiritual reality at the time of application, continues to be a feature of the new covenant community" (405).

9 B. B. Warfield, "The Polemics of Infant Baptism," in *Studies in Theology, The Works of Benjamin B. Warfield* (1932; repr., Grand Rapids: Baker, 2000), 408.

10 Belgic Confession, article 29.

11 We also keep in mind that "particular churches . . . are more or less pure, according as the doctrine of the gospel is taught and embraced, ordinances administered, and public worship performed more or less purely in them" (Westminster Confession of Faith, chapter 25.4). In other words, deficiencies in these areas do not mean that we must necessarily anathematize certain congregations and label them "false churches."

12 Geerhardus Vos, *The Teaching of Jesus concerning the Kingdom of God and the Church* (1903; repr., Dallas: Fontes Press, 2017), 81.

13 R. B. Kuiper, *The Glorious Body of Christ: A Scriptural Appreciation of the One Holy Church* (1958; repr., London: Banner of Truth, 1967), 361.

14 Paul S. Minear, *Images of the Church in the New Testament*, The New Testament Library (1960; repr., Louisville: Westminster John Knox Press, 2004).

Chapter 2: The Necessity of Church Membership

1 Cyprian, *De catholica ecclesiae unitate* 6; PL 4:503. Quoted in Jonathan Gibson and Mark Earngey, eds., *Reformation Worship: Liturgies from the Past for the Present* (Greensboro, NC: New Growth Press, 2018), 51.

2 *Calvin: Institutes of the Christian Religion*, ed. John T. McNeill, trans. Ford Lewis Battles, vol. 2, *Books III.XX to IV.XX* (Philadelphia: The Westminster Press, 1960), 4.1.4. Emphasis mine.

3 Belgic Confession, article 28. Emphasis mine.

4 Second Helvetic Confession, chapter 17 in *Reformed Confessions of the 16th and 17th Centuries in English Translation*, vol. 2, compiled by James T. Dennison Jr., *1552–1566* (Grand Rapids: Reformation Heritage Books, 2010), 848. Emphasis mine.

5 Westminster Confession of Faith, chapter 25.2. Emphasis mine.

6 David Brooks, *The Second Mountain: The Quest for a Moral Life* (New York: Random House, 2019), 11.

7 Westminster Confession of Faith, chapter 1.6. Emphasis mine.

8 See, for example, Jonathan Leeman, *Church Membership: How the World Knows Who Represents Jesus*, Building Healthy Churches (Wheaton, IL: Crossway, 2012); Wayne Mack, *To Be or Not to Be a Church Member? That Is the Question* (New York: Calvary Press, 2007); Peter Masters, *Church Membership in the Bible* (London: Wakeman Trust, 2008).

9 Bruce K. Waltke, with Cathi J. Fredricks, *Genesis: A Commentary* (Grand Rapids: Zondervan, 2001), 261.

10 Mack, *To Be or Not to Be a Church Member?*, 30.

11 Samuel J. Stone, "The Church's One Foundation," 1866.

12 From my lecture notes in a course on ecclesiology taught by Craig Troxel.

Chapter 3: The Blessings of Church Membership

1 In a Presbyterian context, those elders, when they meet and work together, are called a *session*. This comes from the Latin word *sessio*,

which means "to sit." It references the fact that elders are to sit in deliberation and rule over the church body. In some denominational contexts, the elders are jointly referred to as a *consistory*, or simply as an *elder board*.

2   William Ernest Henley, "Invictus," 1875.

3   David Dickson, *The Elder and His Work* (1883; repr., Dallas: Presbyterian Heritage Publications, 1990), 3.

4   The Bible restricts formal leadership in the church to men only. See 1 Timothy 3:2; Titus 1:6.

5   Richard Baxter, *The Reformed Pastor,* edited by William Brown (1656; repr., Edinburgh: Banner of Truth, 2007), 74.

6   The Westminster Confession of Faith says that church discipline is necessary "for the reclaiming and gaining of offending brethren, for deterring of others from the like offenses, for purging out of that leaven which might infect the whole lump, for vindicating the honor of Christ, and the holy profession of the gospel, and for preventing the wrath of God, which might justly fall upon the church, if they should suffer his covenant, and the seals thereof, to be profaned by notorious and obstinate offenders" (30.3).

7   Martin Bucer, *Concerning the True Care of Souls,* trans. Peter Beale (repr., Edinburgh: Banner of Truth, 2013), 78.

8   Bucer, 94.

9   Belgic Confession, article 33.

10   Jason Helopoulos, *Covenantal Baptism,* Blessings of the Faith (Phillipsburg, NJ: P&R, 2021), 30.

11   Geoff Surratt, Greg Ligon, and Warren Bird, *A Multi-Site Church Roadtrip: Exploring the New Normal,* Leadership Network Innovation Series (Grand Rapids: Zondervan, 2009), 93.

12   Westminster Larger Catechism, answer 165. Emphasis mine.

13   Heidelberg Catechism, answer 73.

14   I have written on this theme elsewhere in Jonathan Landry Cruse, *What Happens When We Worship* (Grand Rapids: Reformation Heritage Books, 2020), 136–37.

15   *Calvin: Institutes of the Christian Religion,* ed. John T. McNeill, trans. Ford Lewis Battles, vol. 2, *Books III.XX to IV.XX* (Philadelphia: The Westminster Press, 1960), 4.17.38.

16 Vivek H. Murthy, "Letter from the Surgeon General," in *Our Epidemic of Loneliness and Isolation: The U.S. Surgeon General's Advisory on the Healing Effects of Social Connection and Community* (Washington, DC: Office of the U.S. Surgeon General, 2023), 4; available online at https://www.hhs.gov/sites/default/files/surgeon-general-social -connection-advisory.pdf.

17 Perry Bacon Jr., "I Left the Church—and Now Long for a 'Church for the Nones,'" *Washington Post*, August 21, 2023, https://www .washingtonpost.com/opinions/2023/08/21/leaving-christianity -religion-church-community/.

18 Dietrich Bonhoeffer, *Life Together*, trans. John W. Doberstein (New York: Harper & Brothers, 1954), 19.

19 Bonhoeffer, 20–21.

20 This insight is from Wayne Veenstra, personal correspondence, September 21, 2023.

21 James Bannerman, *The Church of Christ: A Treatise on the Nature, Powers, Ordinances, Discipline, and Government of the Christian Church* (1868; repr., Edinburgh: Banner of Truth, 2016), 97–98.

22 *The Book of Church Order of the Orthodox Presbyterian Church* (Willow Grove, PA: The Orthodox Presbyterian Church, 2015), 161.

23 Richard Baxter, *The True and Only Way of Concord of All the Christian Churches* (London, 1680), 39.

Chapter 4: The Responsibilities of Church Membership

1 Jake Meador, "The Misunderstood Reason Millions of Americans Stopped Going to Church," *The Atlantic*, July 29, 2023, https://www.theatlantic.com/ideas/archive/2023/07/christian -church-communitiy-participation-drop/674843/.

2 John Newton, "We Were Once as You Are," 1779.

3 This is why some churches, while acknowledging the immense blessings that live streams offered during something like a pandemic and lockdown, pulled the plug afterward. They saw that "online church" was actually keeping people from experiencing the community of God's people the way they were meant to. See, for example, Jim Davis and Skyler Flowers, "Why Our Church Will Unplug from

Streaming," The Gospel Coalition, May 27, 2021, https://www
.thegospelcoalition.org/article/why-church-will-unplug.

4 I am thankful to my friend Harrison Perkins for this particular
insight.

5 A. Craig Troxel, "Communion of the Saints: Sharing the Spirit-
Endowed Riches of Christ's Gifts and Graces," in *Theology for
Ministry: How Doctrine Affects Pastoral Life and Practice*, ed. Wil-
liam R. Edwards, John C. A. Ferguson, and Chad Van Dixhoorn
(Phillipsburg, NJ: P&R, 2022), 439.

6 Thomas Schreiner, "How (Not) to Discover Your Spiritual Gifts,"
The Gospel Coalition, July 6, 2018, https://www.thegospelcoalition
.org/article/how-not-discover-spiritual-gifts/.

7 *Calvin: Institutes of the Christian Religion*, ed. John T. McNeill, trans.
Ford Lewis Battles, vol. 2, *Books III.XX to IV.XX* (Philadelphia: The
Westminster Press, 1960), 4.1.3.

8 John Owen, *Duties of Christian Fellowship: A Manual for Church
Members* (1647; repr., Edinburgh: Banner of Truth, 2017), 44.

9 Richard Sibbes, *The Bruised Reed* (1630; repr., Edinburgh: Banner
of Truth, 2008), 23.

10 *The Book of Church Order of the Orthodox Presbyterian Church* (Willow Grove, PA: The Orthodox Presbyterian Church, 2015), 161.

11 Westminster Larger Catechism, answer 160.

12 William Boekestein, "How to Hear a Sermon," Core Christianity,
December 1, 2020, https://www.corechristianity.com/resources
/articles/how-to-hear-a-sermon.

13 Quoted in Sinclair B. Ferguson, *Devoted to God's Church: Core Values
for Christian Fellowship* (Edinburgh: Banner of Truth, 2020), 176.

14 Newton, "We Were Once as You Are."

Questions and Answers on Church Membership

1 Westminster Confession of Faith, chapter 27.3.

2 Westminster Confession of Faith, chapter 25.2.

3 This would be in contradistinction from the minority view of
infant and child participation in the Lord's Supper, known as
paedo-communion. For a classic Reformed and Presbyterian

response to such a view, see Guy Waters and Ligon Duncan, eds., *Children and the Lord's Supper* (Fearn, Ross-shire, UK: Mentor, 2011).

4 Jason Helopoulos, *Covenantal Baptism*, Blessings of the Faith (Phillipsburg, NJ: P&R, 2021), 108.

5 Derek W. H. Thomas, *Let Us Worship God: Why We Worship the Way We Do* (Sanford, FL: Ligonier, 2021), 68.

6 Isaac Watts, "When I Survey the Wondrous Cross," 1707.

7 As Pastor Wayne Veenstra pointed out to me, it's not a spiritual gift that everyone has, since there are some who are homebound due to physical limitations or age. This, though, is but another great reason to participate in the body of the church: there may come a day when you are deprived of the fellowship that you take for granted now.

8 Charles H. Spurgeon, "A Private Enquiry" (sermon, Metropolitan Tabernacle, London, October 9, 1890), https://archive.spurgeon .org/sermons/2184.php.

9 Joseph H. Hellerman, *When the Church Was a Family: Recapturing Jesus' Vision for Authentic Christian Community* (Nashville: B&H Academic, 2009), 1, quoted in Jeremy Linneman, *Why Do We Feel Lonely at Church?*, TGC Hard Questions (Wheaton, IL: Crossway, 2023), 40.